The Bottle, the Breast, and the State

The Bottle, the Breast, and the State

The Politics of Infant Feeding in the United States

Maureen Rand Oakley

LEXINGTON BOOKS
Lanham • Boulder • New York • London

Published by Lexington Books
An imprint of The Rowman & Littlefield Publishing Group, Inc.
4501 Forbes Boulevard, Suite 200, Lanham, Maryland 20706
www.rowman.com

Unit A, Whitacre Mews, 26-34 Stannary Street, London SE11 4AB

British Library Cataloguing in Publication Information Available

Library of Congress Cataloging-in-Publication Data

Rand Oakley, Maureen.
The bottle, the breast, and the state : the politics of infant feeding in the United States / Maureen Rand
Oakley.
p. cm.
Includes bibliographical references and index.
ISBN 978-0-7391-9198-9 (cloth : alk. paper) -- ISBN 978-0-7391-9199-6 (electronic)
1. Breastfeeding--Political aspects--United States. 2. Breastfeeding--Social aspects--United States. I.
Title.
RJ216.R29 2015
649'.330973--dc23
2015007151

Printed in the United States of America

To Madeline and Mike

Contents

Preface and Acknowledgments

I became intrigued with the issue of infant feeding, particularly the controversy that seems to surround public breastfeeding, when I was a nursing mother and heard stories of women being asked to stop breastfeeding or to leave public places. When I discussed the stories with friends, I learned they were not always sympathetic to a right to breastfeed in public, or were quick to point out the need for discretion and the perceived lack of it on the part of some women. These reactions actually kept me from nursing in public most of the time, out of concern for offending others. After ranting about this issue to my husband one day while we were riding in the car, he turned to me and said, "Why don't you write a paper about that?"

I took his advice and wrote a conference paper on state laws protecting the right to breastfeed in public. When I was presenting the paper for a *Women and Politics* section panel at an academic conference, the panel discussant said, "I don't think this should be a feminist issue." This reception was both fascinating and perplexing to me. My paper approached the issue primarily as an issue of comparative state policy and politics, exploring the political activities and media attention that may have led to the passage of the laws in some states.

Yet, I had also argued for a right to breastfeed and viewed it as something anyone who believed in gender equality would support. This right promotes the free movement of *all* women in the public space, regardless of whether they happen to be lactating. I felt I was perceived as a breastfeeding advocate, but I had both breastfed and used formula. I sensed a failure to separate a promotion of the right to breastfeed anywhere from forms of advocacy that used pressure and shaming, which I oppose. As someone who was given formula by a lactation consultant to supplement my child when it was determined she was not getting a full feed, it seemed the *breast vs. bottle* distinction was being overblown in terms of many parents' actual infant feeding experiences in the first year.

After the conference, I began to further explore the debate within feminism on the issue of infant feeding. I discovered that the primary concern of some feminists was about what they saw as pressure to breastfeed by breastfeeding advocates, and corresponding ideas that essentialized women as primarily mothers, due to their biology. For some feminists, activism for the right to breastfeed was associated too closely with pressure to breastfeed, rather than the long-time feminist values of the right to control one's body and the full inclusion of women in public life.

I found many of the women writing on this subject had actually breastfed their own children, sometimes for quite a long time. But because the movement for breastfeeding rights was associated with La Leche League International and breastfeeding advocacy in general, there was concern that this was a push to keep women at home in a traditional role or to add pumping breast milk to the long list of things women must do to be considered good mothers. These early research experiences led me to the conclusion that there are two paradoxes when it comes to breastfeeding promotion in the United States.

The first paradox, which prompted my initial work on the subject, was the presence of strong health messages promoting breastfeeding in the United States, alongside the cultural aversion to public breastfeeding and the continued widespread use of infant formula. The second paradox is that both breastfeeding advocates and their critics actually support both feeding methods more than the rhetoric sometimes indicates. Indeed, most infants are fed a combination of formula and breast milk during their first year of life since the exclusive breastfeeding rate at three months for children born in 2011 was 40.7 percent. This leaves well over half of the babies receiving infant formula or other foods a quarter of the way through the first year. Additionally, lactation consultants help women suffering from primary or secondary lactation failure to supplement with formula without undermining breastfeeding, since banked milk is typically used only for premature and sick infants (Palmer 2013). While formula is typically referred to as the fourth best option for babies, in a typical situation where a child must be supplemented, formula is used by medical personnel assisting the parents, as happened in my own case.

Due to this reality, one would hope that both groups could work together for breastfeeding rights and support, as well as for research on and access to the best quality alternatives for those babies that are not fed human milk. My goal is to start a dialogue between groups that may not always communicate with each other, and to promote a culture where all parents are able to make decisions regarding infant feeding in the best possible environment. This is my hope in writing this book.

This book would not have been possible without the help of many people. I would like to thank the women who took time out of a busy day to share their experiences and their stories with me. I am so grateful to the members of my faculty-writing group who read parts of the book and gave me very useful feedback. I am especially grateful to Marty Malone for organizing the group and providing helpful insights. Bill Prudden, Carolyn Cook, Emily Stetler, and Caitlin Faas challenged and enriched me with their comments and suggestions. Mount St. Mary's University provided support through a sabbatical and financial help with paying for transcription of interviews. My department chair, Mike Towle was a source of support and mentoring on the publishing process. Cheri Baker read chapters and provided ongoing encouragement. I am thankful to an anonymous reviewer whose insightful comments helped me clarify my arguments. Justin Race, my editor at Lexington Books, took an enthusiastic interest in my work from the beginning. He showed great patience with me as I dealt with the challenges of writing my first book. Ashli MacKenzie carefully brought my manuscript through the production process. I am most grateful to her for her accurate work in making corrections to the proofs.

Friends and child-care providers gave loving care to my daughter Madeline while I worked on the early stages of research that eventually became part of the book. I am most thankful to Ann Marie Miller who took care of Madeline in her early years when I first started writing on this topic. My parents, Sandra and Owen Rand, have supported me all of my life and encouraged my academic endeavors; I am so thankful for all the great conversations about life, politics, and breastfeeding. I am eternally gratefully to my husband, Mike, for all his support in everything I do. My daughter, who provided the inspiration for this book, has brought more joy to my life than I ever could have imagined. Thanks, Madeline, for all you have taught me about life and love.

Introduction

Political Scientist, Karen Kedrowski (2008) relates how her own breastfeeding experience illustrates a paradox in the United States surrounding the issue of infant feeding. When she was unable to breastfeed her son after illness and eight days of trying, she was riddled with guilt; yet she was later admonished for nursing her eighteen-month-old daughter at her child care center. She says, "I was a perfectly bad mother; I'm damned because I didn't breastfeed my son and I'm damned because I am breastfeeding my daughter." (Kedrowski and Lipscomb 2008, xii).

Ironically, a second paradox is that the very distinction between breastfeeding and bottle feeding is not as clear as it appears to be. Support for various types of feeding often cuts across groups that appear to be on opposing sides of a rhetorical *breast vs. bottle* debate. In fact, most of those critiquing some of the approaches to breastfeeding advocacy are not against breastfeeding or the right to breastfeed at all, but seek a more supportive culture for all forms of infant feeding (Barston 2012; Blum 1999; Carter 1995). At the same time, health professionals promoting breastfeeding recognize that situations exist where formula may be medically necessary. (Palmer 2009; Sriraman 2013).

In fact, in most situations where infants must be supplemented, medical professionals use formula rather than human milk, which is often unavailable (Neifert 2001, 282, 289; Sriraman 2013). Indeed, when women do not breastfeed for any reason, the hospital provides formula while mother and infant are staying there. If formula were truly regarded as a significantly inferior or dangerous substance, then we would hope improvements or alternatives would be aggressively pursued out of concern for those infants that are not breastfed due to contraindications or other problems. Beyond that, a concern for the health and well-being of any infant who is not breasted should lead not only to substantive policies supportive of maternal breastfeeding, but to greater access to quality alternatives.

This book explores the ways that U.S. culture and policy both promote and undermine breastfeeding, and how feminists, mothers, and activists respond to this paradox. I also explore areas where *breast* and *bottle* are not nearly as distinct as they may appear to be. I use this fact to promote common ground between breastfeeding advocates and critics by proposing an approach that supports women and enables them the opportunity to breastfeed, but that does not shame them when they do not.

Public Breastfeeding and U.S. Culture

Recent media attention has focused on stories in which breastfeeding mothers are asked to move to a restroom or leave an establishment, such as Starbucks, Hollister, or Victoria's Secret. In one story, a woman asked to use the Victoria's Secret dressing room as her son started to cry while she was paying for about $150.00 in merchandise. While the sales clerk who checked her out was nodding her head, another employee said that she could not breastfeed in the store. She recommended an alley outside where no one would see her (it was cold and windy). According to Texas law, the woman had a right to breastfeed her son in the store; instead, she fed him in the mall restroom sitting on a toilet (Morran 2014).

Similar stories have persisted, despite the fact that forty-nine U.S. states now have laws clarifying the right to breastfeed in any public or private place where a woman and her baby have a right to be (NCSL 2015). One problem with the laws, explained by attorney Jake Marcus in an article for *Mothering*, is that most of them do not include any enforcement mechanism, so if women are harassed for breastfeeding, there is nothing they can do about it other than point out the existence of the law. She explains that the laws should include a penalty or path of recourse for the victims; without it, the law is likely to be ignored (Marcus 2007).

Direct action techniques, such as the *nurse-in*, have been used to bring attention to the issue of public breastfeeding. States and the federal government have passed legislation designed to support breastfeeding. The national government also advocates breastfeeding as part of its public health initiatives through the Centers for Disease Control and Prevention (CDC) that regularly collects and reports data on breastfeeding. Yet, the issue of infant feeding is not only political because of government involvement in it, but because breastfeeding, in particular, involves a woman's body. Some argue that public breastfeeding is controversial in the United States because of the sexualization of the breast in media and advertising. One ABC News poll found that 57 percent of the American public disapproves of public breastfeeding (Foster 2013). Interestingly, public breastfeeding appears to be more controversial in the United States than in many other places where modesty for women is much more important and images in the media of sexualized breasts are rare (Palmer 2009).

Feminist Perspectives

While feminists have written a great deal about the objectification of women, the sexualization of women and girls, and the right to control one's body in a reproductive context, the issue of a right to breastfeed has received less attention from feminists, especially prior to the 1990s. Feminists in various disciplines have begun to explore the issue of infant feeding and of breast-feeding in particular. Differing conclusions have been reached about how feminists should respond to breastfeeding advocacy. Many express concern about the focus of advocacy on the individual behavior of women rather than societal structures that make breastfeeding difficult (Blum 1999; Bobel 2001; Boswell-Penc 2006; Carter 1995; Hausman 2003).

A feminist ethic of care can help refocus some of these controversies in a way that can allow us to move forward without getting stuck trying to come up with a truth about breastfeeding. The focus on the individual right to breastfeed and advocacy of breastfeeding that targets the individual woman, without also examining the social context in which women make decisions, devalues the care work they do. While breastfeeding has been viewed as a public health issue, the individualistic approaches taken to breastfeeding pro-motion place all of the responsibility for the health outcomes of the entire population on individual women. An approach that adds social responsibility to individual responsibility is likely to be much more effective.

Tronto (2013) argues,

> From the standpoint of an ethic of care, citizens should be able to expect more from the state and civil society in guaranteeing that their caring needs, and those of their loved ones, will be met. At the same time, citizens must become more committed to producing the kinds of values, practices, and institutions that will allow democratic society to more coherently provide for its demo-cratic caring citizens. (44)

Applied to infant feeding, this could mean citizens would demand the trans-formed social context for breastfeeding that Blum (1999) refers to, as well as a public commitment to find solutions to lactation problems for those who wish to breastfeed. A reevaluing of care and a recognition of its contribution of nurturing democratic citizens would change the way work and public life are organized so that those who desire to breastfeed and work can more easily combine these activities.

While some feminists and breastfeeding advocates work for policies that support families in the care work that we all depend upon, all too often the discussion on breastfeeding has degenerated into an unproductive *mommy war*. This kind of approach is not limited to the supposed *breast vs. bottle* controversy, and is not surprising given the neo-liberal principles of justice being applied. Tronto (2013) points out,

> As long as care is individualized and privatized, it is possible to praise oneself for one's caring and decry the ways in which others care. Such praise and blame will likely follow lines of race, class, ethnicity, region, and religion and will likely make it more difficult to see inequalities as a result of lack of choice. Instead, they may be viewed as the product of others' deliberate bad actions, decisions or ways of life. (102–103)

Left unquestioned are the ways in which public space and work are arranged so that breastfeeding and other caring work are often difficult to combine with paid work.

When work/family balance debates are discussed, they almost always focus only on women rather than men; they assume current work conditions and public/private sphere divisions. Also, in these arguments, common assumptions about the gendered spheres of breadwinning and homemaking are viewed as fixed and timeless, instead of being changeable factors that developed in the United States during the nineteenth century (Williams 2000, 20).

Tronto does not focus on the issue of infant feeding in particular; but her work could be construed as presenting a challenge to breastfeeding since it seeks to distribute care work more equally across gender, as well as class and race lines. The restructuring of care work she proposes would not necessarily have to make breastfeeding more difficult. The more equal division of care work could allow those who wish to breastfeed more time to do so, either through taking advantage of new policies such as family leave and subsidized on-site (and well-paid) child care, or by delegating other types of care work to partners or other individuals.

While breastfeeding has been shown to lead to mothers doing more of the other care work, if attention is given to this imbalance, it is possible to shift the load by assigning non-feeding tasks to others (Rippeyoung and Noonan 2012). Tronto's caring democracy could also allow increased opportunities for less well-resourced women to breastfeed successfully if they so choose, concerns that have been expressed by many feminists (Blum 1999; Carter 1995; Hausman 2012; Wolf 2011; Bobel 2002).

I advocate for a *caring infant feeding advocacy*. My approach to supporting breastfeeding promotes both governmental and non-governmental policies that invest in early childhood as a public good regardless of infant feeding choice. Expanding options through offering paid parental leave, making banked milk more available, providing funding for medical research on primary lactation failure, and improving infant formula are all needed to provide the best context for infant feeding. This would not only make breastfeeding a realistic possibility for the many women who desire to do it but find it difficult for a variety of reasons, but would provide greater societal support to parenting in the early years regardless of feeding choices or parental work situations.

Methodology

Woliver (2002) points out the need to include women's voices when making policy related to reproduction. Women's own stories are the best place to start in order to determine what supports they may or may not desire. I interviewed fifteen women who were currently breastfeeding or had initiated breastfeeding since 1997; their stories are the focus of chapter three. All women had initiated breastfeeding in the hospital with at least one child. Yet, the women represent a range of experiences from direct breastfeeding with no formula use up to three years, to formula feeding before coming home from the hospital with the first child, and consequently, using formula exclusively to feed five subsequent children. I found that all had used a bottle to some extent; some did not use any formula; and many used a combination of breastfeeding, pumped bottles of mother's milk, and formula to feed their infants.

The interviews lasted between one and two hours. I selected respondents from those I had met through observation of La Leche League International (LLL) meetings, as well as other contacts. Most women in the sample had never attended a LLL Meeting, though one was a member and two were leaders. Most interviews were conducted in the greater Washington, D.C./ Baltimore area. I employed a snowball sampling approach, where respondents recommended others I could interview. I focused on capturing a range of experiences. Some women worked full-time while breastfeeding; some did not work outside of the home; and some worked part-time. All of the face-to-face interviewees were white, married, and (though I did not ask directly about income) appeared to be primarily middle class. To get at experiences of a more diverse group of women, I also relied on online sources and blogs such as *Blacktating* and the Black Mothers' Breastfeeding Association website in order to include a broader cross-section of women across race and class.

In selecting respondents for the interviews of women, I used the saturation approach to purposive sampling; I interviewed women who have initiated breastfeeding between 1997 and the present about their goals and experiences. Similarly to what Guest (2006) describes, in the first few interviews I heard of varying experiences with infant feeding but by interview fourteen, I reached a saturation point where the stories began to repeat themselves (Guest, Bunce, and Johnson 2006). As a qualitative research approach, the interviews are not meant to be generalized to the broader population but are done to gain an understanding of women's experiences as part of larger social processes in a specific context (Connolly 1998). While chapter 3 focuses in on women's experiences in particular with feeding their babies, I draw on the interviews throughout the book in addition to document analysis and participant observation.

Additional sources of research for the book include attending monthly LLL meetings over the course of a year, as well as the Beyond LATCH Conference in Chesapeake, Virginia, February 20–23, 2013. I interviewed breastfeeding activists; lactation consultants; Women, Infants, and Children (WIC) breastfeeding staff and peer counselor coordinators; and observed a WIC breastfeeding support group. For chapters 5 and 6, document analysis was conducted on the U.S. Government and American Academy of Pediatrics (AAP) documents.

Outline of the book

Chapter 1 gives a short history of infant feeding in the United States. I outline the rise of the use of formula and prevailing medical advice over time. I explore the rise of scientific motherhood and its connection to the initial decline in U.S. breastfeeding rates across the twentieth century until 1972 (Apple 1987). Breastfeeding rates across time and across groups of women are also examined.

Chapter 2 explores the debate within feminism about breastfeeding advocacy. While some feminists have been supportive of breastfeeding advocacy (Boswell-Penc 2006; Hausman 2003, 2012; Taylor and Wallace 2012; Van Esterik 1989), others are concerned that advocacy will bring pressure on women to stay out of the workforce to breastfeed, or will deem women who do not breastfeed as "bad mothers" (Blum 1999; Wolf 2011).

Smith, Hausman and Labbok (2012) argue that the debate between breastfeeding advocates and feminist critics is at a stalemate because advocates remain focused on health benefits, while feminist critics argue that advocacy ignores the material realities of women's lives and the constraints that make breastfeeding difficult in the American context (3). They call for feminist approaches to advocacy using the Social-Ecological Model (SEM), which focuses on how social influences affect infant feeding practices (Smith, Hausman, and Labbok 7). This approach seeks to address the cultural constraints to breastfeeding, rather than focusing on changing individual attitudes. Drawing on this approach as well as a feminist ethic of care, I advance a *caring infant feeding advocacy,* which promotes social responsibility in the area of infant feeding, in addition to personal responsibility and individual rights.

Chapter 3 explores women's experiences with breastfeeding. As Pamela Carter (1995) points out, the actual lived experiences of women are important to consider in any discussion of breastfeeding and are key to any consideration of policy in order to support women in meeting their own infant feeding goals. Through the interviews, I explore how women have dealt with issues such a breastfeeding in public; switching to formula; working and breastfeeding; and support (or lack of it) by family, friends, and the public. This approach asks women what they think is needed in terms of policy and support for infant feeding and goes from there.

In chapter 4 I provide an overview of state breastfeeding laws, policies, and programs and analyze their effects on breastfeeding rates using statistical analysis. I explore the various laws and practices that affect state breastfeeding rates using data reported by the CDC. While individual level analysis is important, a state level analysis is crucial to understanding this issue due to the vast variation in culture, law, and hospital practices across states. Identifying and zeroing in on practices that are related to higher rates of breastfeeding will help states determine where to place their resources.

I argue that raising breastfeeding rates and duration is an appropriate goal of state officials not because all women have to breastfeed to be good mothers, but because identifying variables that contribute to longer breastfeeding duration means more women will have the support they need to meet their own breastfeeding goals. The importance of this is illustrated by studies that found less than a third of women met their own goal of breastfeeding exclusively for over three months, and that this could be attributed primarily to hospital practices rather than lack of desire to continue (Perrine et al. 2012).

Chapter 5 explores the advocacy of breastfeeding as a public health issue by the AAP and the U.S. Department of Health and Human Services (HHS) through an analysis of policy statements on breastfeeding. I explore the trend toward the use of *risk language* in promoting breastfeeding over formula use. I advocate for a social-policy oriented approach that seeks to transform the social environment into one that is more conducive to breastfeeding and other care work rather than an approach seeking to change attitudes about breastfeeding.

In chapter 6 I explore the activities of grassroots activism supporting public breastfeeding, as well as on-line groups that have arisen to support those who do not breastfeed. The chapter also explores overtly political efforts to lobby government for breastfeeding rights legislation. I suggest ways to build a more sustainable movement focused both on breastfeeding as a civil right, and a caring activity that needs to be valued and broadly supported by social policy.

Lastly, in the conclusion I argue that breastfeeding is still not receiving adequate governmental, societal, and medical support in the United States, given the very strong statements on breastfeeding from the AAP and the HHS. In arguing for more feminist engagement with the issue of infant feeding, I am not asking feminists to engage uncritically in breastfeeding advocacy, but for their voices to further inform current efforts to support women who do breastfeed.

To paraphrase Erin Taylor and Nora Wallace (2012), a feminist advocacy is needed to support women who choose to breastfeed with public policies that help make it possible, without shaming women who cannot or choose not to breastfeed. Building on this approach and incorporating a feminist ethic of care, I argue for a *caring infant feeding advocacy* in which a broad coalition of interests work not only for improved social conditions for breastfeeding, but also for increased medical specialization in human lactation and improved options when maternal breastfeeding is not possible.

Chapter One

Infant Feeding Policy and Practice in the United States

With so much attention on the advocacy of breastfeeding in the last few decades, it is important to reflect on the history of infant feeding practices and its relationship to the medical profession over the course of time. For instance, my own mother explained that she read an article about the health benefits of breastfeeding in the early 1960s when she was pregnant with my brother. Based on this article, she decided to breastfeed him for three months. She did this with little support, reporting to me that no one she knew was breastfeeding. Further, when she told friends of her plans many said, "I don't know why you would want to bother with that." She also mentioned that she never nursed in public and that she was instructed to offer a supplementary bottle after each feeding, which she did per her doctor's instructions.

It is important to note that my mother did not work outside the home at the time and that my father drove the only family automobile to work each morning, so breastfeeding out of public view would not have required too much of a change from her usual routine. She explained that she was able to meet her goal of nursing my brother for three months without too much difficulty. However, when I asked if she also breastfed me, she explained that when she gave birth to me in late 1965, she told her physician of her plans to breastfeed for three months again; he told her that she would not be success-ful nursing a newborn with a two-year old "running around." She took his advice and used formula to feed me.

Another story illustrates changes over time in hospital practices related to infant feeding. I mentioned the topic of my research to some coworkers in a break room during lunchtime. One woman explained that she was given a pill in the hospital to dry up her milk when she gave birth in the 1970s. I inquired as to whether anyone asked her if she intended to breastfeed. She said, "No, they just gave it to me. They never asked." Another coworker weighed in and said, "When I gave birth in the late 1980s, it was all about the breastfeeding." This chapter gives a brief history of breastfeeding trends and practices in the United States and sheds some light on the major shifts in infant feeding practices that these stories illustrate.

Major Breastfeeding Trends

In the late nineteenth century and the beginning of the twentieth century, most infants in the United States were breastfed at birth by their mothers, though supplementation had become common and was considered a public health concern by 1900. A general decline in the breastfeeding rate continued until its low point in 1972, when 22 percent of infants were breastfed. The breastfeeding rate began to increase again in 1975, from 33 percent to almost 60 percent in 1984. The rate dropped a bit in the late 1980s and then increased again during the 1990s, returning to 60 percent again by 1995 (Wright 2001, 1).

The breastfeeding initiation rate has increased to 79.2 percent breastfeeding at birth in 2011. While rates at three and six months have been significantly lower, these rates have increased over the past several years (CDC 2012; CDC 2014). In 2011, 49.4 percent of infants were breastfed at six months and 26.7 percent were breastfed at twelve months. As for exclusive breastfeeding of infants, 40.7 percent of infants were exclusively breastfed at three months of age in 2011 and 18.8 percent were exclusively breastfed at six months (CDC 2014).

There continues to be a great deal of variation in breastfeeding rates across demographic groups of women. Historically, white women have been more likely to initiate breastfeeding and this difference still holds; but the biggest increases in the 1990s occurred among minority women, low-income women, WIC participants, and women with the least amount of formal education (Wright 2001, 3). While working is often cited as a barrier to breastfeeding, Wright (2001) points out that it is important to remember that breastfeeding rates were dropping when workforce rates for women were lower, at mid-century; breastfeeding rates increased again during the time when more women were entering and staying in the workforce while their children were young.

Women who were not employed outside of the home were more likely to initiate breastfeeding in the early 1980s, but this is no longer the case. Duration does appear to be affected by work, as women working full-time are more likely to wean before their children are six months of age (Wright 2001). This is not surprising for the United States as women typically take off six weeks of work or even less for the birth of a child, often without pay depending on the policies of their employers. Since 1994, the Family and

Medical Leave Act (FMLA) requires some employers to give twelve weeks unpaid family leave after the birth or adoption of a child, but employers with under fifty employees are exempt. Ludden (2013) points out that 40 percent of the workforce is not eligible for leave under the FMLA.

The Rise of Scientific Motherhood

In the late nineteenth and early twentieth century, a practice referred to as scientific motherhood developed that centered on the medical supervision of infants for proper development (Apple 1987). As Ward puts it, "while women continued to be children's primary care providers, both they and the medical community believed that they needed expert advice to perform their duties successfully" (Ward 2000, 31). Both Ward and Apple address how beliefs about women contributed to a focus on developing a suitable substitute for breast milk in response to a rise in infant mortality, rather than on helping women breastfeed their infants. However, some local public health departments in large cities did launch their own breastfeeding campaigns (Wolf 2003).

Doctors T. B. Greenly and J. A. Work viewed non-breastfeeding mothers in a negative light, arguing that they were too selfish and foolish to properly feed their own children. Poor women were seen as too immoral and wealthier women as too concerned with fashion and wanting to move about freely, to properly suckle their children (Ward 2000, 32). What was left unexamined, however, was the culture that often kept nursing women out of view, even inside their own homes where they often did not control even that private space (Carter 1995). There were also many myths about women's milk being affected by emotions or curdled by physical and sexual activity (Apple 1987).

While beliefs of the time held that mother's milk was healthful for the baby, many physicians also believed that women's actions could affect the quality of milk and that they could not be counted on to follow healthy behaviors. Infant care manuals written by doctors became popular in the twentieth century such as *The Care and Feeding of Children*, by L. Emmett Holt (first published in 1894 and remained in popular use until 1940) and *What You Ought to Know About Your Baby*, by H. L. Mencken, whose book was based on Holt's approach. This approach concentrated on rigid feeding schedules and minimizing contact with the mother's skin to prevent infection. However, Holt was not the first to suggest a regimented, scheduled approach to feeding. As early as the 1500s, male physicians in Europe were writing about the issue of gastrointestinal problems in infants and high infant mortality. The problem was attributed to overfeeding, so strict schedules and limited feeds were recommended (Apple 1987,104; Ward 2000, 32).

Given this, it is not surprising that after the professionalization of medicine in the mid-1800s, and the development of the subfield of pediatrics around 1900, some of these ideas were resurrected. Supervising infant feeding became a major part of pediatricians' practices. With the medical field dominated by men, much of the knowledge that had been transferred from woman-to-woman previously lost prestige and was devalued. However, Apple makes clear that women and doctors were both agents involved in the change that took place. In concluding her work on the social history of infant feeding, she writes:

> The history of infant feeding from the late nineteenth century to the mid-twentieth century documents the growing commercialization and medicalization of infant care, raising questions about the interaction of science, medicine, and commerce and illustrating the complexity of cultural change. Above all, it reveals that in their search for healthful infant care, women participated in a redefinition of the maternal role. The ideological, economic, and medical factors that transformed motherhood earlier in the century continue to influence the lives of American women and our sisters throughout the world. (183)

It should be noted that the public health focus on breastfeeding in the last several decades is not completely new. In nineteenth century France, the use of wet nurses was so popular that there was a push to get mothers to nurse their own children. Similarly in the United States by 1900, a practice of feeding cow's milk to young infants had led to a problem of infant deaths from dehydration caused by diarrhea. One problem was that unmodified cow's milk was not suitable for the digestive system of an infant, and the other problem was contamination and spoilage of milk that could occur between the farm and the home, especially in the summertime due to lack of refrigeration (Wolf 2003).

This triggered health department campaigns across the country to encourage women to nurse their children. Also in response to these deaths, maternalists in the first decades of the twentieth century opposed women's wage labor and artificial feeding as part of a push to lower infant mortality rates (Blum 1999, 24). According to Jacqueline Wolf (2003), increasing numbers of women began to feel bottle feeding was necessary and that their milk was insufficient. Both middle-class and working-class women sought out medical advice for infant care, so the trend of scientific mothering had already begun. It became increasingly more common to bottle feed milk-modified foods under the direction of a physician during the late nineteenth century (Apple 1987). Even by the 1880s, some babies were weaned or given supplemental cow's milk prior to three months of age. This contrasts with the colonial era in which infants were ordinarily fed at the breast for two years or more, typically through the child's second summer (Wolf 2003). Even prior to the early weaning trend, the affliction cholera infantum (infant diarrhea) was known as the "disease of the second summer" because children frequently developed it when weaned and introduced to cow's milk.

In addition to women and physicians, another group contributing to the complex changes taking place in infant feeding were chemists. During this time period, several chemists were involved in creating commercial foods using cow's milk as a base, but modifying it to suit an infant. Liebig's Food was sold beginning in 1869 in the United States, and Nestlé's Milk Food was widely available in the 1870s. While Liebig's formula for modifying cow's milk was considered to be based on science, it was not easy to prepare, which led the chemist Gustav Mellin of England to develop Mellin's Food. While it was easier to prepare, Mellin's Food needed to be mixed with both milk and water. Thus, the problem of poor refrigeration and contamination of milk, which posed such a danger to infants, remained. Nestlé's, on the other hand, needed only to be mixed with water. One ad for the product in 1888 emphasized this fact stating, "Nestlé's Food is especially suitable for infants in hot weather. In the case of Cholera-Infantum, Nestlé's Milk Food is alone to be recommended" (Apple 1987, 12).

Coinciding with the decrease in breastfeeding rates during the first half of the twentieth century was a decline in homebirths. In 1920, only about 20 percent of women birthed their children in a hospital in the United States, but this number increased to 80 percent by 1950 (Apple 1987, 159). Also from 1946 to 1950, breastfeeding initiation had fallen to about 25 percent. Rates in this range continued until 1972 (Wright 2001). Apple examines how the trend away from maternal nursing and toward formula use was part of a larger medicalization of pregnancy and childbirth. According to Apple, "the hospital fostered an ideology of scientific motherhood, the need for scientific and medical expertise in the successful rearing of infants" (1987, 159).

It is important to understand the broader context of the medicalization of childbirth and childrearing. A number of medical advances greatly improved health, lowering infant mortality rates during the entire twentieth century. Antibiotics were developed during World War II and vaccinations became available for many childhood diseases, from which so many parents had lost children. With these changes also taking place, any declines in health due to a reduction in breastfeeding rates may have been masked by the positive trends from these other advances. In this context, one can see how parents may have taken infant feeding advice as part of this scientific expertise (Kedrowski and Lipscomb 2008, 27).

Breastfeeding rates have been influenced by a number of factors in addition to scientific motherhood. Kedrowski and Lipscomp sum it up this way:

> We see a fusion of a norm of good mothering attached to class status, coming into contact with a logic of medicalization. As these factors coalesced over the course of the twentieth century, and as they eventually hooked up with wom-

en's entrance into the work force in the latter part of the century, and with the increasing commercialization of the erotic breast during the same time period, they had the overall effect of driving down breastfeeding rates in the United States. (26)

Wright points out, however, that while some of the decrease in breast-feeding rates frequently gets associated with participation of mothers in the workforce, the relationship is complex; there is no available data with which to test this hypothesis systematically. Data from the last few decades shows a relationship between working and breastfeeding, but it has shifted over time. Early in the 1980s, Wright (2001) points out, women were more likely to breastfeed if they were not employed outside the home at all. But by the end of that decade, there was no difference in initiation of breastfeeding between these two groups. There was a difference in breastfeeding duration for mothers employed full time, which continues. Full-time working mothers have been more likely to wean from the breast before their infants were six months of age (Wright 2001).

Wright and Schandler (2001) argue that the natural childbirth movement of the 1960s and 1970s and its effects on the management of childbirth likely explain much of the increase in breastfeeding rates during the 1970s and early 1980s. LLL was founded in 1956 while breastfeeding rates were still on the decline, but it became increasingly well-known during the natural childbirth movement period (Ward 2000). Wright and Schanler (2001) point out that this was actually a time of unprecedented rates of women with young children entering the workforce, yet breastfeeding rates dramatically increased from 22 percent to 60 percent during this time. The natural childbirth movement led to more women attending childbirth preparation classes, receiving information about breastfeeding from medical personnel, and fewer receiving anesthesia during childbirth, or being separated from their infants for more than six hours after birth; all factors that have been associated with increased breastfeeding (Wright and Schanler 2001, 422S).

Global Infant Feeding Controversy

As early as the 1950s, Dr. Catherine Wennen pointed out problems she encountered in Nigeria due to the aggressive advertising and promotion of infant formula. She encountered babies sick from being unnecessarily fed formula in an environment where clean water was often not available, and incomes could not support long term use of formula. In 1972, Dr. Derrick Jelliffe also wrote about this problem in an article called "Commerciogenic Malnutrition" (Palmer 2009).

Media attention to the issue continued to grow; in 1974, Mike Muller and the organization War On Want produced *The Baby Killer*, a report about the tactics used for advertising and marketing infant formula in developing nations. The public was especially disturbed to learn about promotion inside hospitals that had been going on for decades by baby nurses who were often salespersons dressed as nurses hired by formula companies to sell their products (Muller 1974).

The reports brought attention to the issue of the aggressive advertising of formula in developing nations. But Gabrielle Palmer (2009) argues in the newest addition of her book, *The Politics of Breastfeeding*, that the film *Bottle Babies* by Peter Krieg had the biggest impact in 1975 because of the stark images of a woman using dirty water to make a bottle and of clearly malnourished infants. The Nestlé Boycott began in 1977 and continued until it was suspended for a time in 1984, when Nestlé agreed to follow the World Health Organization's (WHO) International Marketing Code (the Code).

The Code was adopted by the World Health Assembly in 1981, without the vote of the U.S. delegates who were under instructions from the State Department to vote against it. The Code regulates the advertising and marketing of infant formula in developing nations. The Nestlé boycott was re-launched in 1988 and continues to be coordinated by the International Baby Food Action Network (IBFAN) due to Nestlé's continued practice of providing hospitals with free and reduced costs formula supplies, which IBFAN argues violates the Code (Palmer 2009; Muller 2013).

These global events may also have contributed to increased breastfeeding rates in the United States due to increased media attention to the subject of breastfeeding. While Muller (1974, 2) emphasized the differences between formula use in developed and developing nations and stated that it is a perfectly adequate infant food with "proper preparation and hygiene," the controversy nonetheless brought more attention to the issue of breastfeeding, which was at its lowest point in the United States in 1972 (Wright 2001). At the same time, articles on the medical benefits of breastfeeding also began to appear in the 1960s and 1970s (Palmer 2009).

The federal government began to promote breastfeeding as a public health initiative in the 1980s. In 1984, the Surgeon General held a workshop on Breastfeeding and Lactation in Rochester, New York. Galson writes, "The workshop represented a milestone in efforts to improve maternal and child health, and highlighted breastfeeding as a public health priority" (Galson 2009). The breastfeeding initiation rate was then at 59 percent, and now has reached 79.2 percent for 2011 births (Galson 2009; CDC 2014).

In order to coordinate efforts to create a supportive environment for breastfeeding in the United States, the United States Breastfeeding Committee (USBC) was formed in 1998 from what had been the National Breastfeeding Leadership Roundtable. The formation of the committee followed the format laid out in the UNICEF innocent declaration of 1990 in order to promote and protect breastfeeding globally (USBC 2014). It is a nonprofit organization with many member organizations, including LLL International, the AAP, and the Black Mothers' Breastfeeding Association, to name a few. Members also include regional breastfeeding coalitions from across the United States. Several governmental health agencies are also represented as non-voting members.

Overview of Federal Legislation Related to Breastfeeding

Federal legislation passed in 1999 (as an amendment to a U.S. postal appropriations bill) protects breastfeeding in public in a federal building or on federal property if the woman and her child are otherwise authorized to be present at the location. This includes museums, courthouses, federal agencies, and national parks throughout the nation that are owned or maintained by the federal government. Additionally, U.S. Representative Carolyn Maloney (D-NY) has introduced the Breastfeeding Promotion Act during many sessions of Congress. In 2009, the bill was also introduced in the Senate for the first time with Jeff Merkly (D-OR) sponsoring the bill, and was reintroduced in 2011 (HR S1463). The 2011 bill would have amended the Civil Rights Act of 1964 to prevent employment discrimination against breastfeeding women by clarifying that the Pregnancy Discrimination Act (PDA) of 1978 applies to lactation and breastfeeding.

While the bill did not pass, some provisions of the legislation were adopted into law through Section 4207 of The Patient Protection and Affordable Care Act (ACA) of 2010, which amended the Fair Labor Standards Act (FLSA), or federal wage and hour law. The amendment requires employers to provide reasonable break time and a private, non-bathroom place for nursing mothers to express breast milk during the workday for one year after the child's birth. The provision does exempt businesses employing fewer than fifty workers if it presents a significant burden. If the 2011 bill had passed, it would have extended workplace protections to salaried workers who breastfeed on breaks and at lunch. These workers are not currently covered under provisions in the ACA (USBC 2010). The USBC supports the proposed Supporting Working Moms Act, also sponsored by Maloney and Merkly, that would extend these workplace provisions to support twelve million salaried employees, including public school teachers (USBC 2013).

This chapter has reviewed the major trends in breastfeeding practices and policies in the United States that led to a decline in the practice during the first half of the twentieth century and the eventual return to the higher rates of breastfeeding we see today. While the issue of breastfeeding has been largely framed as a public health issue, some have called for it to be viewed as a reproductive rights issue, a civil rights issue, or both, while others have opposed advocacy of breastfeeding altogether. The next chapter takes up the issue of feminist perspectives on breastfeeding advocacy and policy.

Chapter Two

Feminist Perspectives on Infant Feeding

The subject of breastfeeding has not received as much treatment in the women's studies and feminist literature as other aspects of childbirth and motherhood; but beginning in the late 1980s, scholars in various disciplines began to take on this subject to a greater extent (Apple 1987; Blum 1993, 1999; Bobel 2001; Carter 1995; Hausman 2003; Ward 2000; Boswell-Penc 2006). While clearly a women's issue by its very nature, breastfeeding has been a difficult subject for feminists. It empowers many women on the one hand, but leaves women vulnerable to biological determinism on the other hand. Linda Blum (1993) points out that "breastfeeding provides a wonderful lens magnifying the cracks and fractures in our construction of the late-twentieth century mother." She further explains, "As an experience of intense interdependence between mother and infant, breastfeeding is easily romanticized; yet at the same time, the present social context makes breastfeeding extremely difficult for many women" (291).

According to Blum, pregnancy, childbirth, and nursing are all challenging issues because American feminism has been focused on equality objectives. Under this ideal, law and policy treat women no differently from men. Policies that promote breastfeeding or guarantee rights to breastfeed in public recognize the biological differences between men and women. Therefore, some feminists fear these policies will be used to exclude women, especially in the workplace, as have some protective labor policies of the past. This problem is known variously in feminist theory as the equality versus difference, equality versus sameness, or the equality versus fairness dilemma (Blum 1993, 1999; Carter 1995; Galtry 2000; Ford 2006). Blum (1993) argues that breastfeeding poses issues that are even more difficult to deal with than pregnancy and childbirth because it often occurs over an extended period of time (291).

In her earlier work, Blum (1993) argues for a feminist preference for breastfeeding, despite the difficulties of overcoming the tendency toward biological determinism, because of the satisfaction it can bring women. In her 1993 article, Blum makes the case "to privilege our access to breastfeeding as a sensuous, noncommodified experience of our bodies" (297). She asserts that women should not sacrifice this experience, but should work to make it possible for more women. She states, "In privileging breastfeeding, I argue for a transformed social context for mothering, one in which the pleasurable physical and emotional aspects can be widely available, genuine choices for women" (Blum 1993, 306). In other words, by using her breasts to feed her infant, a woman repossesses them from the patriarchal culture that turns them into sexual objects for the sheer pleasure of men.

In her later work that focuses on a variety of women's infant feeding experiences across race and class, Blum shifts her position on feminist privileging of breastfeeding due to the varied experiences of women she encountered in her field research. Yet, she maintains her position that a focus on the social context of breastfeeding is necessary so that women in a variety of circumstances are able to make decisions that are best for themselves and their families. Blum (1999) argues that there is no one true meaning of breastfeeding for women, asking:

> Can breastfeeding be in women's interests in the twenty-first century? . . . There is no one answer and no position free of danger. To nurse our babies at the breast may offer a way to revalue our bodies and force a public reevaluation of caregiving—or—at the same time, it may represent acquiescence to dominant regimes of self-sacrifice, overwork, and surveillance (198).

Blum (1999) further concludes, "Whether bottle or breastfeeding, or some hybridized combination using genetically engineered animal milks, I hope for a twenty-first century of flourishing, rounded, multi-shaded mothers" (201).

Like Blum, I agree that we need to reject the idea that there is a single experience shared by all women when they breastfeed. But we need to work to create a public space where the embodied woman is fully included and not marginalized because she may be lactating. In the current context, those who might otherwise feel empowered by the experience may not feel that way because they do not have the social support they need. We won't know what the experience will be like for women until we create that environment. I argue that in order to improve the social context for breastfeeding, a broad based political movement is needed advocating for not only policies supportive of breastfeeding, but of parenting and care work more generally. In order to unearth some of that common ground, I review feminist insights on breast-feeding practices, advocacy, rights, and policy.

Feminism, Breastfeeding, and Public Spaces

In arguing for an increased feminist engagement with breastfeeding, Bos-well-Penc makes the case that feminists are well-situated to engage on the issue of breastfeeding because, as she puts it, "Feminists have critiqued cultural models that teach women to distrust our physical embodiment and see our bodies in narrow ways, as sexual objects in the service of male heterosexual fantasies, but have not tended to venture into the fields of breastfeeding and child nourishment" (Boswell-Penc 2006). Increasingly, some academic feminists have discussed sexualization of the breast in Western culture and how it shapes the social context for breastfeeding. In her study of breastfeeding women in Great Britain, Pamela Carter (1995) illuminates this problem:

> Breasts are acceptable in public if they are presented (clothed or not) in ways which correspond to non-reproductive (hetero) sexuality. Links between motherhood and sexual breasts are clearly disturbing unless firmly held within a discourse of mothering in a 'private' place. These dichotomies intersect with each other so that women's bodies are constantly scrutinized, by themselves, and others, to make sure than they neither deny sexuality, nor flaunt it. It is through the daily construction of femininity that women's bodily experiences are mediated. (128)

According to Carter, at the turn of the twentieth century, breastfeeding was nearly always relegated to the private sphere, despite the medicalization of infant feeding and the emphasis on the health benefits and lower mortality rates by public health workers:

> Breastfeeding developed this aspect of its place within private and public discourses as part of alarm in the last century and in the early part of this, about infant mortality rates. Breastfeeding mothers had to stay at home and do their duty in private but feeding itself became a public issue, subject to professional surveillance. (131)

Post-second wave feminism, women are in public life more than ever before, yet this aspect of many women's lives has never really been widely accepted in the public space in the United States. Rima Apple (1987) points out that alternatives to breast milk were viewed as liberating women, as the Pet Milk ads stated in the 1930s, a woman can "Take the Baby and Go!" What is left unexamined is why public space was not and often still is not considered open for breastfeeding women and their children. The ad is not surprising given that the sexualization of breasts in Western culture increased beginning in the 1930s (Carter 1995; Newson and Newson 1963).

Many feminists have tended to focus on expanding women's opportunities in public life; yet the primary focus has been on their exclusion from pursuits once seen as primarily for males, such as voting, holding office, higher education, and the workplace. These are not the only ways in which women have been limited and proscribed. Some scholars have explored the ways in which women have tried to navigate breastfeeding while having an active life in the public sphere without running afoul of cultural notions of appropriate behavior for women (Stearns 1999; Maclean 1990).

Given this history of breastfeeding not always being accepted in the public space in the United States, what is the lived experience of women who do breastfeed in public? Stearns (1999) explores this in her study of women in Sonoma, California. None of the women in her sample reported being asked to leave a public place, but all "carefully managed" their public breastfeeding and put a great deal of care into being discreet. They gave particular attention to making sure men did not misinterpret their actions as sexual in nature. She concludes:

> The perceived need to hide breastfeeding and proceed with discretion effectively keeps some women home and out of public life more than they would be otherwise. It is this very fear that breastfeeding will exclude women from public life, essentializing women's otherness from, difference from, men that may explain why breastfeeding has not been framed as a feminist issue with much frequency. . . . But certainly a feminist social agenda would include allowing women to use their bodies in ways they wish. (Stearns 1999, 323)

It is worth pointing out that Stearns' study was done in California, which is in one of the most supportive regions for public breastfeeding and has higher rates of breastfeeding than most states (Hannan et al. 2005). More attention to the experiences of women breastfeeding in the public space is needed so that a comparison can be made across regions. In chapter 3, I explore women's experiences of breastfeeding primarily on the East Coast and draw many of the same conclusions.

While some may argue that the women in Stearns' sample were overly concerned about men's perceptions of their public breastfeeding, given that none were ever confronted, polling data suggests that overwhelming majorities of fathers of infants felt that public breastfeeding was unacceptable in a 1992 Pediatrics poll (Kedrowski and Lipscomb 2008). Even among fathers of breastfed infants, 71 percent said it was unacceptable, while 78 percent of fathers of infants who were not breastfed disapproved of the practice. However, a 1995 Gallup poll found that 57 percent of parents of breastfeeding infants felt that breastfeeding in public should have legal protection (Kedrowski and Lipscomb 2008). Another poll from 2004 showed 57 percent of the public responded that women should not breastfeed in public (Hannan et al. 2005). It is difficult to know the extent to which a lack of acceptance of breastfeeding in public prevents women from breastfeeding, but certainly these statistics show that for a practice so highly recommended as healthy for women and their children, it has continued to be regarded as problematic when done in public.

Since the typical breast-fed child nurses roughly every two to three hours, these public attitudes present some significant challenges for active women who wish to nurse their children. Stearns brings attention to why the right to breastfeed in public needs to be viewed as a feminist issue. While feminists and other scholars have critiqued breastfeeding advocacy out of concern that it pressures women to breastfeed without recognizing constraints on this decision (Blum 1999; Law 2000; Wolf 2011), there has not been as much feminist attention to the environment for women who do decide to breast-feed. Stearns correctly points out that feminism needs to pursue freedom of movement in the public sphere for women and their children regardless of their nursing status. It is crucial to decouple the idea of supporting the right to breastfeed from pressuring women to breastfeed without addressing cultural problems. The intertwining of these ideas has led to a continuation of the status quo where women are strongly encouraged to breastfeed, and then frequently find the culture unsupportive.

It seems straightforward that Stearns' argument that women using their bodies as they wish to feed their own children is something that a feminist social agenda should include. This position is sometimes seen as being un-supportive of parents who use formula. There is no reason that this must be the case. Similarly, advocating for the right to procreate does not mean one must be unsupportive of those choosing not to have a family. Support of the right to homeschool does not mean one does not support those who send their children to school for their education. Most likely, the concern is due to the belief that this stance will be taken as support only for breastfeeding in the current social context. Concern within feminism about women being essen-tialized by their biological characteristics underlies much of the consterna-tion with this subject. Yet, failure to engage in a discussion of this issue outside of academia leaves intact a status quo in which women are urged to breastfeed for at least a year. But when some attempt to do so, they find public life unwelcoming and work situations challenging.

Perspectives on Breastfeeding Advocacy

Blum's (1993) suggestion in her earlier work to reclaim the experience of breastfeeding on women's own terms can be seen as resistance to the con-flicting notions of femininity. Young argues that many women revel in the experiences of pregnancy, childbearing, and breastfeeding, which are derived from women's own biology (Young 1990; 74). She argues that we can value some dimensions of women's experience and the different values they may represent from the dominant masculine culture, while still resisting the dichotomy. Blum's subsequent work on infant feeding across race and class shows that some women may still not choose to breastfeed even if the public space were more welcoming. Their decision could be due to other reasons involving the use of networks of relatives and other women who help with parenting and who may not be supportive of or familiar with breastfeeding (Blum 1999).

Supporting an atmosphere that allows true freedom and self-determination in these matters should be the goal of feminists and others. Feminists should oppose mother-guilt or coercion to either breastfeed or use formula, but they can and should work to improve the social context for breastfeeding. This can be done alongside breastfeeding advocates wherever there is common ground. It often goes unnoted that many breastfeeding advocates speak out against a negative, mother-blaming approach, as Jamie Lynne Grumet, the USBC, and others have done. (Grumet 2012; Smith, Hausman, and Labbok 2012; USBC 2012).

The goal must be to work toward a society that values and supports the caregiving work people do for those who are in a dependent stage of their lives. Dependency is something we all face at the beginning and often at the end of our lives. Therefore, creating a society that helps support caregivers, including breastfeeding work, should be desirable to feminists who have long focused on how the false dichotomy between the public and private sphere ignores the essential work of caregiving often done by women both inside and outside of the home (Kittay 1999; Tronto 2013; Woliver 2002).

Several scholars have explored the ways in which La Leche League International (LLL) both challenges and embraces the dominant culture through its philosophy on mothering (Blum 1993, 1999; Bobel 2001; Ward 2000). In her qualitative study of the organization, Christina Bobel points out that LLL is a rare place in our culture where motherhood is truly affirmed. On the other hand, Bobel (2001) and Blum (1993) both express concern for the naturalistic view of motherhood taken by LLL that emphasizes the infant's constant need not just for mother's breast, but "for all of her." Bobel also points out that the membership of the LLL chapters she studied highlights the class, marital status, and race/ethnicity bias of the broader population of breastfeeding women. Most of the members she interviewed were white, middle class or higher economic status, and married. This is reflective of the demographic characteristics of women most likely to breastfeed. Bobel (2001) points out, "sadly any health benefits which breastfeeding may confer are not evenly distributed" (146).

These patterns are not surprising, given that the social constraints on breastfeeding will impact some groups more than others. Women who are most likely to have support at home and at work will have more opportunity to breastfeed their infants than other women, due to the current context in the

United States where most workers do not have access to paid family leave. Interestingly, Blum (1999) finds differences between the working-class white and African American women she interviewed. For the most part, the white working-class women in her sample very much wanted to be married and to breastfeed, but encountered many obstacles to these goals, leading many of them to feel that their bodies, and often their baby's fathers, had failed them. On the other hand, most African American women in Blum's sample had different perspectives, though some of their experiences were similar to those of the working-class white women.

In general, Blum found the working-class African American women employed a model of independent mothering that was not as focused on marriage, and that they tended to reject breastfeeding as the goal or ideal in the first place (Blum 1999). Blum's field research shows that even if some barriers to breastfeeding are removed, this will not necessarily lead to all women breastfeeding. These findings contribute to the shift in her position from a feminist privileging of breastfeeding to a position that there can be no one fixed meaning of breastfeeding for mothers or for feminists (Blum 1993, 1999).

It is important to point out, however, that there is a breastfeeding movement among African American women that has not received much attention in the academic literature. Katherine Barber, for example, founded the African American Breastfeeding Alliance in 2000 to address the needs of black women and the isolation they may feel when they breastfeed in their communities. Another group based in Detroit is the Black Mother's Breastfeeding Association, which is a member of USBC. In Milwaukee, the African American Breastfeeding Network formed in 2008 to support women's efforts to nurse their babies. The Detroit and Milwaukee groups are easily found online and more information about Barber's efforts to increase breastfeeding rates in the African American community and to improve health outcomes can be found on her website at http://www.kathibarber.com.

According to Wright (2001), "The recent increase in the breastfeeding rate has been greatest among black women using the WIC program."(4) Since then, the trend continues upward, according to Donya Currie's 2013 article in *The Nation's Health*, an online publication of the American Public Health Association. Currie (2013) points out that the percentage of African American women who breastfeed, while still lower than for other groups, has doubled since the year 2000.

Given the upward trend, the apparent lack of African American women attending LLL meetings noted by some scholars may be due to reasons other than a rejection of breastfeeding. As Barber puts it, many African American women felt some breastfeeding support guides and groups were not relevant for them because of specific experiences they had in common that women in the dominant racial group may not share or understand. This led Barber to write *The Black Woman's Guide to Breastfeeding* where chapter 8, entitled, "Our Breastfeeding Heritage," addresses the historical legacies of slavery and the post-slavery period. She makes a case for black women to reclaim the experience of breastfeeding for both the benefits to themselves and their children. She emphasizes the higher infant mortality rates of black children and other health statistics as well as arguing that breastfeeding can help bring these rates more in line with those of other children (Barber 2005). While she does not address feminism directly in this particular book, other breastfeeding advocates in the African American community have addressed the relationship between feminism and breastfeeding.

For example the blog, *Blacktating: Breastfeeding News and Views from a Mom of Color* was started in the year 2000 by Elita Kalma (2010) to specifically address the concerns of African American women. While feminists have written about racial differences in breastfeeding and the danger of breastfeeding advocacy further marginalizing minority women, or stereotyping them as bad mothers, there has been less attention to the breastfeeding movements within the minority community. Kalma responds to some writing within academic feminism in her blog, *Blacktating*. For example, in a November 5, 2010, post she says this about Joan Wolf's (2007; 2011) critique of breastfeeding advocacy:

> Are we seriously still asking women to believe that breastfeeding isn't compatible with feminism? Wolf seems to be . . . Many women come to the conclusion that bottle-feeding was not as freeing as they were led to believe it would be. And isn't the harassment of nursing moms in public that we hear about every day, the judgment of our choices from friends, family, and healthcare providers alike, the pushback to any accommodations that are made for us, just as worthy of feminist discourse? Where are the scholars writing about that? (Kalma 2010)

This response shows that more attention to perspectives on feminism and breastfeeding from minority women and minority women scholars in particular needs to be included in the debate among feminists. Kalma repeats the same argument we hear from Stearns—that the right to breastfeed whenever the need arises is a concern that is certainly relevant to feminism, as it involves women's ability to exercise control over their bodies; something feminists have long advocated. This remains an important area for feminist exploration given the frequent focus on race and class in theoretical and empirical feminist work on breastfeeding; but it is crucial to include a range of perspectives from the African American community.

Jules Law offers a critique of the conclusions drawn from the medical research upon which breastfeeding recommendations and advocacy are often based, arguing that modest findings in the most apparently neutral studies often end with a strong endorsement of breastfeeding. He attributes this approach to the unexamined cultural assumptions of a nuclear patriarchal family where women are presumed to be the primary caregivers, thus influencing recommendations to breastfeed (Law 2000, 419). Law seeks to put infant feeding into its context where decisions about a host of child-rearing practices are made, all of which include some risk. Indeed, he says that there is no risk-free way to raise a child. Families must consider the benefits of paid employment for either one or both parents as well as many other factors in caring for children and supporting families.

Others have similarly critiqued the current approaches to breastfeeding advocacy for preventing a more equal division of labor and for an over-emphasis of marginal infant medical benefits to the exclusion of other family and career considerations (Barston 2012; Rosin 2009, Wolf 2011). Wolf (2011), for example, frames breastfeeding advocacy as part of a broader neoliberal risk culture where "individuals practice a regulated autonomy and have responsibilities to the collective" (61). She goes on to say that "Neoliberal citizens, in short, take care of themselves" (Wolf 2011, 61). She argues that an ideology of total motherhood has developed that "stipulates that mothers' primary occupation is to predict and prevent all less than optimal social, emotional, cognitive, and physical outcomes; that mothers are responsible for eradicating every imaginable risk to their children . . . and that any potential diminution of harm trumps all other considerations in risk analysis as long as mothers can achieve the reduction" (Wolf 2011, 72). Wolf wonders how much would be made of the health benefits of breastfeeding if it were fathers who did this task. She argues that this total motherhood approach "suggests that when specific threats require sacrifice or intervention from others—fathers, communities, government—they are more likely to be discursively invisible, rationalized, or framed as something other than risky" (72).

On the other hand, Boswell-Penc (2006) points out that the formula as liberation idea is a false one because someone is still doing the feeding. While it could be the father in the case of formula or expressed milk, it will often be other women who are more oppressed than the middle-class women who are liberated so that they can go back to work; however, problems of low paid caregivers and a lack of benefits in this line of work are rarely considered in this context. Gabrielle Palmer has also made this observation (2009). An approach that focuses on societal support for caregiving through better pay and benefits for child-care workers, as well as better family leave benefits would help reduce the need to make such constrained choices. Going beyond a rights approach to provide substantive support is necessary if opportunities to breastfeed are to be equalized across socioeconomic and other demographic characteristics.

Hausman (2012) points out that both breastfeeding advocates and their critics need to get beyond arguing over the medical advice and whether it overstates the medical evidence and focus on why so many women have to choose between breastfeeding and paid employment in the first place. Since both sides of the breastfeeding advocacy debate often agree on this point, they ought to seek to alter that situation through activism for policy change. The truth is that women should be able to combine breastfeeding and a career or to be able to breastfeed their babies wherever they are just because they want to, regardless of their reasons and the extent of any medical advice. As Wolf (2011), states women who choose to breastfeed have many reasons for their decision and that "women might well choose to breastfeed if public spaces, including workplaces, were more favorable" (150). One can organize in support of policies that transform the social and work space for women, while at the same time critiquing some of the approaches used in breastfeeding advocacy or even the advocacy itself.

Indeed, in many Organization for Economic Co-operation and Development (OECD) nations, women can breastfeed in the first year if they so choose, much more easily than in the United States:

> The incidence of exclusive breastfeeding and its duration tends to be higher/ longer in countries with long periods of maternity/parental leave, such as the Nordic countries, Hungary, and the Czech Republic, but the relationship does not always hold as British and Irish experiences illustrate. Other determinants of breastfeeding include infant characteristics and cultural attitudes towards breastfeeding. (OECD 2009)

It is important that in defending and supporting women who do not breastfeed because of work or other considerations, we do not end up settling for the unfavorable conditions that may have facilitated that decision. It is not a zero sum game. One can advocate for supportive policies for breastfeeding without condemning those who do not breastfeed. Indeed, longer and/or paid family leave and flexible work arrangements are changes that can benefit all parents and help us all invest in the work being done to nurture our future citizens.

In her book, *The Paradox of Natural Mothering*, Bobel (2002) argues that in the natural mothering movement of which breastfeeding and extended breastfeeding is often a part, women both rebel against the popular culture and accommodate patriarchy at the same time. Bobel also points out the fact that most of the women in her sample were middle-class and white; they were focused on changing the consumerist culture, but not as much through social activism, as through focusing on their own families' lifestyles. Some argue that a lack of concern for racial and class inequalities in breastfeeding may arise from the fact that women were told in the last century to trust scientifically formulated alternatives to breastfeeding and not to trust their bodies, and now the culture still trusts only some women's bodies (Blum 1999; Bobel 2001, 146). This is a valuable insight; but without action to change the social context, the status quo continues and the conditions for those who wish to breastfeed are not addressed. It makes the most sense to both oppose individualized pressure and shaming, while at the same time supporting public or private policies that make breastfeeding more possible for those who wish to do it.

If a more supportive environment can be created for all women through public policies, medical practices, and education of the public (not just mothers), then this may help to even the playing field and could be part of a feminist agenda. Avoiding a judgmental, mother-blaming approach is obviously essential to any feminist support of a right to breastfeed. Moving from a focus on changing individual behavior alone to one that includes the social context, as Blum (1993, 1999) urges, is a step in the right direction. As Boswell-Penc (2006) observes, it is going to require feminist involvement and activism in order to bring this about.

Hausman identifies a heavy use of education and advocacy rather than a women's rights approach as a major shortcoming of public health approaches to promoting breastfeeding. She states, "Rights frameworks point us toward the structural elements influencing personal decisions and practices and they assume that individual intention, will, and fortitude are insufficient to address such constraints" (Hausman 2012, 19–20). She argues for governmental and non-governmental supports that go beyond education and focus on reducing the gender inequities that make it challenging for women to breastfeed (Hausman 2012). Hausman asserts, "We cannot pretend that individual practices will make up for a sociocultural context inimical to breastfeeding, because our expectation that mothers can supersede their material and ideological realities contributes to the very constraints on breastfeeding that we want to change" (23).

Because many breastfeeding advocates are lactation consultants and LLL leaders involved with helping to support women one-on-one who are currently breastfeeding, the focus tends not to be directly on public policies.[1] This creates a scenario where both breastfeeding advocates and their critics are focused more on the current situation for individuals, with advocates helping individuals to navigate current constraints and critics focusing on the constraints as valid reasons not to breastfeed. The trouble is that this approach does not focus on changing conditions to make breastfeeding less challenging for those who have found it so. For example, in terms of national organizations, both the National Organization for Women (NOW) and the USBC support paid family leave, but this needs to be translated into grassroots social activism if real change is to occur.

Feminist Analysis of Court Cases and Legislation

One prompt for legislative attention to breastfeeding has been the uneven judicial response to cases involving the rights of breastfeeding women. Some feminists argue that further civil rights legislation is necessary to protect breastfeeding in the same way that the Pregnancy Discrimination Act (PDA) was needed to protect pregnant women from discrimination (Galtry 2000; NOW 2006). The Breastfeeding Promotion Act, which was introduced many times by Representative Carolyn Maloney (D-NY), would have done this had it passed Congress. It was last introduced in 2011. While a small portion of this act was incorporated into the Affordable Care Act, it only covered pumping for some employees and did not extend the PDA to include breastfeeding and establish a civil right for lactating women.

In terms of employment issues, courts have rejected the notion that breastfeeding is within the scope of the PDA or that it constitutes discrimination under Title VII of the Civil Rights Act of 1964 (CRA). The Sixth Circuit ruled in *Wallace v. Pyro Mining Company*[2] that breastfeeding was not a medical condition related to pregnancy and childbirth (Kedrowski and Lipscomb 2008). Also in *Martinez v. N.B.C. Inc.*[3] the court declined to "elevate breast milk pumping . . . to a protected status" (Eldredge 2005, 889). Additionally, suits brought under the Americans with Disabilities Act (ADA) have been rejected by the courts, which have consistently ruled that breastfeeding does not constitute a disability within the ADA (Eldredge 2005, 898).

The issue of breastfeeding discrimination has not reached the United States Supreme Court. In *Dike v. School Board of Orange County Florida*,[4] the Fifth Circuit held that breastfeeding was a fundamental right under the U.S. Constitution but, nonetheless, ruled in favor of the school board that did not allow Dike to leave school or have someone bring her child to the campus for breastfeeding during her breaks when her infant refused to take a bottle. According to Kedrowski and Lipscomb (2008), "the Court ruled that the school board's competing interests in preventing disruptions in the educational process and limiting liability were equally valid" (71). Some courts have also ruled that breastfeeding is not protected by existing sex discrimination laws such as Title VII of the CRA and the PDA. Since the Court has recognized fundamental rights that have included the right to marry, procreate, use birth control, and engage in adult consensual sexual activity, some legal scholars speculate that the Supreme Court may find breastfeeding to be a constitutional right. However, even if this is the case, constitutional rights are not absolute and may be subject to limitations in the face of competing interests, as the Fifth Circuit found in *Dike* (Kedrowski and Lipscomb 2008).

In a state of Ohio case regarding the issue of public breastfeeding, the Sixth Circuit court ruled in *Derungs v. Wal-Mart Stores Inc.*[5] that Ohio's

Public Accommodations Statute (OPAS) prohibiting discrimination on the basis of sex was not violated by Wal-Mart. Three women brought suit against Wal-Mart after they were each asked to use the restroom to breastfeed their children on three separate occasions in three different stores. The circuit court affirmed a district court ruling that applied the comparability analysis that is used at the federal level to interpret Title VII of the federal CRA to OPAS. This interpretation assumes sex discrimination can only occur when women are treated disparately from men. If the plaintiffs can find no comparable class of men that was treated differently, they cannot be successful in the suit (Whelan 2005).

Feminist legal scholars have observed that the comparability analysis in the case of sex-specific conditions leads to the ridiculous conclusion that the policy did not discriminate because it did not allow people of either sex to breastfeed their children in Wal-Mart stores. Since the restrictions are aimed at an activity that only women are engaged in, they are not viewed as treating one sex differently than the other; therefore, no discrimination occurred in the eyes of the court. The Ohio legislature adopted a public breastfeeding law in 2005 in direct response to this ruling (Whelan 2005).

The understanding of sex discrimination only as a lack of sex neutrality in which people of one sex are favored over the other has obviously meant that treatment based on conditions unique to women has not been considered discriminatory. In the case of *General Electric Company v. Gilbert*,[6] the United States Supreme Court ruled that differential treatment of pregnant women, by excluding pregnancy from an employer's disability plan, was not sex discrimination because pregnant and non-pregnant persons are treated differently, not men and women. This case prompted Congress to amend Title VII of the CRA through the PDA of 1978 to clarify the meaning of sex discrimination to include the condition of pregnancy and related medical conditions. In doing this, Congress was rejecting the idea that discrimination based on conditions specific to women is not sex discrimination. Whelan (2005) argues that the *Derungs* decision shows that the courts have not extended the logic of the PDA to other sex-specific situations such as breastfeeding, but have clung to the pre-PDA or *Gilbert* definition of sex discrimination. Using similar logic, the Fourth Circuit ruled that the denial of a female employee's request for six months unpaid leave to breastfeed her child did not violate Title VII of the CRA in *Barrash v. Bowen*.[7]

Whelan argues that the comparability analysis is faulty and outdated logic, and that the courts should extend the reasoning of the PDA to other sex-specific activities such as breastfeeding; Galtry (2000) makes a similar argument. Whelan contends that the narrow interpretation of sex discrimination allows employers to use a characteristic that only women possess as a pretext for discrimination based on sex. Since the 1990s, U.S. Representative Carolyn Maloney (D-NY) has been introducing legislation to amend the PDA to include breastfeeding (Kedrowski and Lipscomb 2008). The national chapter of NOW has also called for this remedy (Galtry 2000). Thus far, while other policies have been adopted involving insurance coverage of breast pumps and workplace pumping accommodations for some employees, the PDA still does not include breastfeeding. It is important to point out that any legislation that is passed to protect breastfeeding rights needs to have enforcement provisions and penalties in order to be effective (Marcus 2013).

In her article, "The Quest for a Lactating Male: Biology, Gender and Discrimination," Eldredge argues that while state legislation to protect breastfeeding is helpful, a state-by-state approach may lead to uneven protection for women. She argues that the ideal approach would be a federal law similar to the PDA but equating discrimination with differential treatment of women for any biologically unique characteristic, rather than just breastfeeding. This seeks to address the problem of the courts using the comparability analysis in any case that comes up that involves sex-specific traits, unless there is specific legislation providing protection for that trait. This would eliminate the need to pass federal legislation for each sex-specific condition. Eldredge argues that "a combination of litigation, legislation, and public pressure is needed to achieve the ultimate goal of Title VII" (Eldredge 2005, 900).

The dominance of rights discourse in the United States has led to an emphasis on the legal equality doctrine (requiring gender neutrality in law) over the fairness doctrine (requiring sensitivity to sexual difference), which has led us down the path of passing even more specific rights legislation. As was seen in the *Derungs* court ruling, the dominance of the legal equality doctrine, rather than the fairness doctrine, has allowed much sex discrimination to continue because of sex-specific situations such as breastfeeding. Ford points out that a legal equality approach "has a solid basis in liberal democratic theory, making it an appropriate solution to the problems women face in gaining access to the public sphere, but it is not without its problems" (Ford, 12). Ford further argues that "the fairness doctrine addresses some of these problems inherent in the legal equality path but presents a different set of unique challenges for men and women seeking gender equality" (12). Focusing on equal treatment of men and women has gained some success because it does not challenge the underlying assumptions of liberal ideology and its characterization of the autonomous individual. Since this characterization ignores biological and social differences in the status and needs of men and women, it leaves room for the pregnancy discrimination seen prior to the PDA and for the harassment and discrimination faced by some breastfeeding women. As Eldredge points out, the status quo leaves open the possibility that women can be discriminated against for any biological difference not already covered specifically in law. As one attorney, breastfeeding advocate and mother I interviewed, put it: this kind of approach to rights "gives women the right to be men."

The approach Eldredge advocates may be seen as a fairness approach, rather than an equality approach, because it would mandate that women be accepted fully into the public space and workplace as embodied women, and that their biological characteristics not be treated as "unique." Ford points out that scholars are divided on whether an equality approach or a fairness approach should be applied to women's rights issues (Ford 2006). Because the rights framework of liberalism is so dominant in United States culture, this makes the prospects for success of a fairness approach tenuous. The perceived danger of the approach is the way protections for women may be interpreted in a society that ignores these differences and sees each individual as autonomous and unencumbered. Supporters of traditional gender roles may view the "need for special rights" as a sign that women indeed belong in the private sphere, at least when they become mothers. They are only "special rights" if one does not believe embodied women and men both deserve to move freely in public space and to combine work and parenthood without attempting to change or deny part of their biology.

While I would argue that support for the right to breastfeed can certainly be considered a part of the movement toward family-friendly workplaces and public spaces, Law (2000) and others have argued that infant-feeding decisions are child-rearing rather than child-bearing decisions. Galtry argues that this distinction has been referred to as a "bright-line" by Kay (1987, 80) but that it may require renegotiating to allow women who wish to combine paid employment and breastfeeding to do so (Galtry 2000, 300). I think this goes to the heart of the challenge with feminist debates about breastfeeding because it is simultaneously something that only women can do and also something that all women do not do.

Eldredge (2005) argues that the "breastfeeding as choice" view of the courts has been problematic. She writes, "Some argue that breastfeeding, infertility treatments, or even conception are a woman's 'choice,' and therefore that protection for these activities should not exist" (894). She furthers argues that "to frame breastfeeding as a choice, and to require women to choose between breastfeeding and work, is no different that requiring women to choose between pregnancy and work—a choice that Congress and the courts have clearly rejected" (894). Additionally, Hausman (2003) argues that breastfeeding needs to be advocated as a right similar to pregnancy, building upon the feminist health movement. She aptly captures the problem of the way the conflict is currently deadlocked, writing, "To admit women into the public sphere on the condition that they give up the physiological uniqueness of maternity to be there is wrong. It is also wrong to suggest that because a few well-resourced women can breastfeed, all women can and therefore should" (228).

Because society values and depends on the work women do when they give birth, legislation has been passed to enable them to do this and be part of the paid labor force. Similarly, if society values the work women do when they breastfeed their children, as the strong public health messages appear to demonstrate, then we all need to support these contributions. On the one hand, when a woman wants to combine working and breastfeeding, there is an argument made that these are simply her personal choices; but when government documents refer to breastfeeding as a public health issue, her choices become a matter of public concern. Rather than continue to urge women to do something that may be a challenge in current conditions, an appropriate public health policy will work toward substantive policies to support breastfeeding.

Eldredge's argument helps lead us to what is often left unquestioned in legal debates about sex equality—the origin of the neutrality approach. This approach derives from liberal thought's conception of the self and its relationship to other human beings. As Glendon points out, the individual under this construction is "a self-determining, unencumbered individual, a being connected to others only by choice" (Glendon 1991, 48). In this construction, the state must be neutral. This has led to a tendency to follow a legal equality approach (or sameness) rather than recognizing biological differences such as the fact that only women give birth and breastfeed. Also ignored is the fact that all are dependent and cared for at some point in their lives. This includes both those aspects of child care that have traditionally fallen to women through social custom as well as those that derive from biology, such as childbirth and breastfeeding. Under the individual rights framework, the individual has no ties of dependency to others that are not entered into voluntarily; thus, liberal man is decidedly male. When this conception of individuals is applied to men and women in determining policy, these existing inequalities between the sexes are reinforced and reproduced. We see this situation in the case of breastfeeding when women are told that giving breastfeeding up is the price they pay for wanting a career.

Where Do We Go From Here?

Pateman (1988) has argued that feminists need to reject the dichotomy of sameness versus difference since it basically accepts the liberal conception of the citizen as male, then tries to go from there to rectify the situation by allowing differences from the male standard or ignoring them as if they did not exist. Carter (1995) discusses a third model of diversity advocated by scholars as a solution to the dichotomy of equality and difference without focusing on biology (Lewis and Davies 1990; Scott 1988; Gatens 1988). Carter explains that this model rejects the limiting view of the citizen as an unencumbered male in liberalism and argues that "the range of obligations and activities over an adult's lifetime are recognized and pre-existing in-equalities are compensated for" (28). Carter also asserts, "What has become clear is that we can neither simply ignore sexual difference, nor build a whole world upon it" (228).

The diversity model offers some promise for understanding the best ap-proaches for feminist advocacy of breastfeeding rights and related family leave policies. One can imagine a collection of policies that could come from this line of thinking. The current Family and Medical Leave Act (FMLA), for example, allows some employees to take up to twelve weeks of unpaid leave. This policy is gender neutral and could be taken to breastfeed an infant, or for a father to care for an infant. It also is used to take time off work by any parent, male or female, after the adoption of a child (Ray 2008). While the FMLA is quite limited because it is unpaid and much shorter than leaves offered in other OECD nations, it recognizes a diversity of situations and is not based on biology (Kedrowski and Lipscomb 2008).

Some may argue that policies like the FMLA and state paid family-leave policies in California and New Jersey have the same effect as maternity policies based on biology since they are taken more often by women than men; therefore, employers may still try to avoid hiring the more FMLA-prone women. Palmer (2009) has responded to this argument by pointing out that the nations that have the most generous maternity benefits are those in which women have become the most equal. She cites Sweden and its ample maternity benefits as an example. However, keeping policies versatile recog-nizes that care work can be done in an array of situations by a variety of individuals depending on what they have decided is best in their particular situation. Also, this approach can help support movement toward a more equitable distribution of care work as Tronto (2013) has advocated. Kedrow-ski and Lispscomb (2008) have argued for expansions to policy that allow paid leave and exempt fewer employees than the FMLA currently does.

While additional state and federal legislation to protect breastfeeding rights may help decrease some barriers to breastfeeding, an individual rights approach has put us on a treadmill of continuously needing to amend legisla-tion to clarify rights as the shortcomings of the neutrality approach come to light. This allows critics to charge that "special rights" are constantly being created. Some argue that protective legislation that follows the fairness doc-trine also leaves women vulnerable to the accusation that the need for these protections shows that they cannot compete equally in the public sphere. Again, this reasoning continues to work from a male standard. What is ig-nored is that this ideal worker is not only assumed to be male, but is assumed to have someone else caring for his children and even his own needs (Aguilar 2012).

How can feminists improve the conditions in which women find them-selves so that they can meet their own breastfeeding goals, whatever those may be? In writing about the problem of toxins in breast milk, Boswell-Penc (2006) explains that instead of a singular focus among environmentalists, breastfeeding advocates, and feminists on improving the environment so that it is safe for all women to breastfeed, the issue gets largely ignored because no one wants the information to keep women from breastfeeding. Similarly, since feminist and breastfeeding advocates agree there is a lack of societal support for breastfeeding, there is an opportunity to forge coalitions across perspectives to work for policies that would have a broader benefit for society by providing greater support to parenting more broadly.

Another crucial reason to include feminist voices in advocacy is to continue to improve support for breastfeeding so that it meets women's needs without the shame (Taylor 2012). Some feminists have pointed out that public health must return to a focus on changing the environment to remove barriers so that some women, especially in lower-paid occupations, won't need to go to "heroic measures" (as Bernice Hausman puts it) in order to breastfeed (Hausman 2012). For example, some low-wage workers describe pumping on breaks in their cars or pumping in restroom stalls with hand pumps. While public health and medical approaches will be examined more fully in chapter 5, this feminist perspective needs to be brought to all advocacy efforts.

In uniting to support a common cause, feminists should join with other groups to press for governmental and non-governmental policies and practices that help support mothering and parenting more broadly. This helps address the perception among some women that feminists devalue mothering and care work by focusing primarily on equal treatment and workplace issues. By engaging more fully in discussions about breastfeeding and pushing for supportive parenting policies, feminists can appeal to broader groups of women and offer support to women in the area of infant feeding.

Feminists who advocate an ethic of care reimagine a society in which care is valued, supported, and less gendered (Kittay 1999; Tronto 2013; Woliver 2002). This offers a way to reframe debates about breastfeeding advocacy and allow breastfeeding to be valued as part of broader efforts to support care work that bridges across types of feeding and gender of the caregiver. Woliver (2002) argues for "a caring jurisprudence that does not frame issues as zero-sum struggles in which one side wins all and the other side loses everything. This caring jurisprudence would draw from the ethic of justice and the ethic of care which incorporates nurturance into the human condition" (163).

While it is unlikely that the prevailing medical advice to breastfeed will change soon, it is important to see breastfeeding rights and family-leave policies as supporting opportunities regarding infant-feeding so that the decisions truly are ones parents can make based on their own given situation, rather than lack of societal or employer support. Carter (1995) argues that "this absence of feminist engagement with the politics of infant feeding has left virtually untouched a dominant construction of infant feeding problems as involving an irrational, if natural, woman who needs to be told again and again why breast is best" (1).

Kedrowski and Lipscomb (2008) propose a democratic feminism as a way to bridge the gap between breastfeeding advocates and critics of the advocacy. They argue for promotion of a right to choose to breastfeed, rather than a duty to breastfeed or a right of an infant to be breastfed. By supporting breastfeeding more substantively, women who wish to choose it but face barriers, may be able to meet their goals. Kedrowski and Lipscomb (2008) argue that is can be done without making breastfeeding a duty. This avoids the problem of assuming a "one size fits all" approach and leaves the decision to the parent. However, they also move beyond a traditional notion of individual choice by recognizing the social context and need for supportive policies in order to make it possible for many women to breastfeed (Kedrowski and Lipscomb 2008).

By protecting the right to choose to breastfeed, we need to move beyond the understanding of choice currently used by the courts, where breastfeeding is seen as a mere choice among various feeding options. We need to remember that while women can decide not to breastfeed, they do not make decisions to lactate. When most (but not all) women give birth, their bodies produce milk for their babies. Having a career or wanting to go out in public should not mean they must stop this process and purchase formula, though they certainly may choose this option. However, this is exactly the way the courts have interpreted choice in infant feeding by rejecting breastfeeding as a condition related to pregnancy under the PDA. Lactation is most certainly a condition related to pregnancy since at least 95 percent of women who give birth produce milk (Neifert 2001). While some women experience primary lactation failure due to medical conditions like insufficient glandular tissue, breast cancer, or hypoplastic breast syndrome, the vast majority of women produce some colostrum and/or milk. In the United States, 79.2 percent of women giving birth in 2011 engaged in some amount of breastfeeding (CDC 2014; Neifert 2001; Smith 2013).

Viewing the infant feeding issue through the lens of both an ethic of care and a civil rights framework will provide the best approach to supporting whichever kinds of infant feeding methods women and their families use. While women need the right to breastfeed outside of a private place if they are to be fully included active members of society, legal rights alone are not enough. A commitment to care work by the broader community through workplace and government policies to support caregiving will make breastfeeding a more viable option for less privileged women.

This approach also offers a way out of the current situation where women often combine a career with all of the other work they do to keep the household running. Hochshield has called this the second shift, and some scholars have argued that adding pumping breast milk would constitute a third shift (Blum 1999; Hochshield 1988; Barston 2012). Many women want to combine work with breastfeeding and they should be able to do so. Civil organizations have recognized this as well. LLL now frequently offers evening meetings; the latest edition of *The Womanly Art of Breastfeeding* (LLL 2010) has much more information about combining breastfeeding and working. With increasing numbers of women breastfeeding and women with small children in the workforce, Kedrowsi and Lipscomb (2008) point out:

> Consequently, these two trends are on a collision course. More and more women want to work outside the home and breastfeed their children. Thus, we see at the same time a collision between the public and the private spheres and confluence of traditional and modern forms of mothering that neither the liberal feminists of the 1970s nor the La Leche League founders of the 1950s foresaw. (8)

Of course, the trends need not be on a collision course and are not in many countries where paid family leave is readily available to most workers. Many feminists and others favor longer paid family leave to support the important and very necessary care work done in families that every human being depends on (NOW 2012; Kedrowski and Lipscomb 2008; Bowell-Penc 2006, 120). Paid family leave would be supportive of those who choose to breastfeed exclusively, but it also benefits a much broader range of individuals—men and women who would like to take more time off from work to care for family members.

By supporting policies that make more options possible, one is not endorsing a specific choice in infant feeding but allowing real choice to take place. Paid family leave, while it has costs, reduces the problem articulated by Boswell-Penc (2006); more marginalized women perform care work while middle-class women work at jobs with benefits. Of course, this is not to say this work will not still be needed or that wages and benefits for childcare workers should not also be addressed; but providing adequate paid family leave provides more options to parents who need or want to both provide income and engage in raising the next generation of citizens.

An ethic of care approach helps break the deadlock over whether getting involved in advocating for breastfeeding rights and supportive public policies essentializes women based on their biology. This approach recognizes that all human beings need care at some point in their lives. In the case of feeding at the breast, this particular work must be done by women, but this does not mean it should continue to be devalued; rather policies and norms need to change in ways that will support and value this work while also enabling men to engage in other kinds of care work more easily. The family-leave policies of Demark and many other OECD nations do this by allowing each parent to take extended leave to care for a child (Ray 2008). This provides the governmental support so that norms can develop that spread responsibility for care more equally between men and women and across the community. A system of insurance that spreads the cost of paid family leave broadly across society recognizes that democracy depends on care work and spreads the cost out across earners— all benefit from the early investment in human capital, just as they do from the societal investments in public education.

Feminists have disagreed about the extent they should get involved in promoting policies to support breastfeeding because of their association with breastfeeding advocacy, which has sometimes taken a naturalistic view of women. This has led to a tendency in the academic literature to critique traditional breastfeeding advocacy and to call for an improved social context for breastfeeding without really advancing a mechanism by which to do this. In the remaining chapters, I argue that feminists, parents, and breastfeeding advocates must forge an alliance in order to transform the public space and work space into a welcoming place for all women regardless of how they feed their infants.

NOTES

1. Public health approaches are addressed further in chapter five. Lactation consultants, RNs, and La Leche League leaders I spoke with and interviewed were supportive of social approaches as well, but their own day-to-day involvement with the issue is on the individual level of breastfeeding support.

2. 789 Supp.867 (US Dist. 1990)

3. 49 F. Supp.2d 305 (SDNY 1999)

4. 650 F. 2d. 783 (1981 U.S . App.)

5. 141 F. Supp. 2d 884 (SD Ohio 2000)

6. 429 US 125 (1976)

7. 846 F.2d 927 (1988)

Chapter Three

Infant Feeding on the Ground: Women's Voices

After researching the subject of breastfeeding policy for several years, in early 2013 I began interviewing women about their infant feeding practices in order to hear firsthand what they experience when they make decisions about infant feeding and carry them out.[1] Woliver (2002) discusses the need to include women's voices and stories when making policies related to reproduction. In this way, women can share what needs they may have for policy, rather than policymakers deciding what is needed. The goal is to discover how policy can support care work without disempowering women in the process.

In this chapter I seek to discover what women experience and what kinds of support or advocacy they feel are needed. The women all initiated breastfeeding in the hospital with at least one child (as 79.2 percent of women in the United States did in 2011). Their methods represent a broad range of infant feeding experiences including primarily formula use, feeding at the breast, exclusive pumping, and a mixture of methods with the same infant.

Decisions about Breastfeeding or Formula

When I asked women how they came to the decision to breastfeed their children, many said they had read about the health benefits of breastfeeding. Many interviewees reported that their mothers had breastfed, which influenced their decision to do so. For example, Cathy said, "I read about it. My mom was a big proponent of breastfeeding. She nursed five kids, so she was very pro doing it. She would talk about it and encourage me." Cathy also illustrated another theme that was common among women I spoke with; she explained, "I just thought it was the healthiest and natural thing to do."

Heather also said her mother had breastfed her. She stated, "I just knew I wanted to breastfeed them. It's so natural." Kristine said, "We were breast-fed. I think I always knew without knowing that I would breastfeed."

Sometimes, women's early experiences prevented them from breastfeeding or from continuing to breastfeed. Erin D., who used formula exclusively with five subsequent children after experiencing latching issues with her first son, explained it this way:

> He didn't latch right so from then on with the other five I just didn't breastfeed and that's how I decided. I feel I can bond just as well. I did breastfeed for two weeks. I actually felt I bonded better once the stress of trying to get him to latch was gone . . . I mean it is the most natural and the way our bodies were designed, but if your body does not function the way it was designed and you have to go another way, I don't think it should be a big deal. I shouldn't be made to feel like a second-class citizen.

Public Breastfeeding

While none of the women I spoke with could remember being confronted while breastfeeding in public, some felt they could sense disapproval; this led some to avoid public breastfeeding as much as possible. Only one woman reported that her spouse had concerns about her breastfeeding in public. But others reported that men would look at them and that they and their spouses were surprised and offended that someone would ogle a woman who was breastfeeding her baby.

I found that one group of women I interviewed avoided breastfeeding in public and never felt comfortable with it, while another group breastfed in public often. I did not find a pattern here related to whether the women were working outside the home, or even with how long they breastfed. However, when I probed further, I found that even those who felt fairly comfortable breastfeeding in public gave attention to being discreet and were more at ease in some places than others. Similarly to Stearns (1999), I found that most women "carefully managed" breastfeeding in public. For example, Michele, who was nursing her son said,

> I have nursed in public. It doesn't bother me. It depends. It's a day by day thing you know if we get up in the morning and he doesn't eat well I have to pump so, like for instance while we are here, if I just pumped a whole six ounces of milk, then I may just feed it to him in the bottle, but I have no problem if I'm in JC Penney's sitting aside, putting a blanket on and nursing. I nurse a lot in my car when I take my daughter to dance class; the studio is so small . . . It's natural, you know, it doesn't . . . I don't even think about it. If I am in church and I need to nurse I'll nurse.

Michele mentions that she covers up with a blanket, so I ask her to say a little more about her experiences breastfeeding in public. She went on to explain how her husband feels:

> My husband, he's a little old fashioned. I remember we were about to get our pictures taken for Christmas cards. He's there and he's got the blanket going around me. I'm like, seriously, if anybody's trying to look at my booby, I don't care. I'm sure they've seen one before.

She explained her take on some of his concerns saying, "He's just so worried. He's very supportive; but he's not worried someone will be offended, but worried someone's gonna see. Yeah. He doesn't care if someone gets offended cause he knows we're doing it for the right cause."

While all of the women in my sample viewed breastfeeding as natural and healthy, all put some thought and planning into public breastfeeding. The theme of discretion was expressed by almost all of the women, whether they were fairly comfortable with public breastfeeding or not. Like the women in Stearns (1999) study, they resisted cultural norms that see the breast as primarily sexual by asserting themselves and feeding their children. Yet, most also covered with a blanket to meet cultural norms about women not showing the breast in public, even when covering was difficult in some situations or with some infants.

Some of these challenges are illustrated by Michele's experience. While Michele seemed to be fairly comfortable with breastfeeding in front of others, she also perceived that sometimes others were not comfortable. She explained that the attention to modesty she felt was necessary with feeding in public sometimes made it more of a challenge than feeding at home:

> You have to catch yourself, because at home you're so free . . . like that shocks some people, so I really have to catch myself with covering up, you know. We don't use a blanket at home so whenever I put a blanket on he's like grabbing at it and pulling it down. I don't think . . . there are times I'll get frustrated, but its not because I'm uncomfortable. It's because now I'm all set up and he's getting fussy or he doesn't stay on or he just wanted to snack and pull off, snack and pull off, snack and pull off and that's frustrating especially when you're in public. I don't mind when it's at home; when you're in public, you're situating everything and picking up the blanket and it's just . . . so that part is frustrating and that's when I'm like okay I'm going to go to my car and I'm okay with that. I like it; I got the radio and it's quiet. There's no distraction.

This statement shows that while Michele does see breastfeeding in public as "no big deal," there's a lot of ritual involved in breastfeeding in the public space, even though she does this often. This was somewhat common among those who did breastfeed in public, although some gave it more thought than others. Michele mentions retreating to her car in some situations, which was a frequent practice with many of the women I interviewed. While cars parked in public lots are not completely outside of public view, they seem to provide women with their own space where they feel more relaxed when breastfeeding.

Even among those who breastfed for at least a year, frequently in public, there were places where women were less comfortable or were sure to be very discreet. Like Stearns (1999), I found that breastfeeding in restaurants or near male coworkers or male strangers were some of the least comfortable places for women. One mother, Heather, who breastfed all four of her children for one to two years said, "I'm sure there were times when I was a little more uncomfortable depending on where I was." When I asked her which places were the least comfortable, she replied, "I'm embarrassed in a church, restaurants, the mall." When I asked her if she just fed them there anyway she explained, "Yes. Absolutely. My baby was hungry and that's how they ate." Heather conveyed a strong commitment to breastfeeding her children, but also a concern for modesty. When asked about her husband's feelings about breastfeeding in public, she answered, "He was so supportive and he knew I was as discrete as I could be."

In describing how they were discrete in public most women talked about covering with a blanket or intentionally wearing certain types of clothing that would hide most of the breast. Heather explained, "I probably just used a little white diaper. The nursing tops, they had the little flap that you could pull it out discreetly." When I asked Christine, a college professor, if she ever had a problem with breastfeeding in public, she said, "No. I never had any issue. If we were in a restaurant or something, I had big sweaters; I would just kind of do it, you know. No. I don't think I ever had anyone make a comment." She also talked about nursing in front of work colleagues saying, "I think if I was around male colleagues, I felt uncomfortable; but with female colleagues I didn't mind."

While none of the women reported being confronted by strangers about breastfeeding in public, their stories show the thought and care they put into breastfeeding to avoid being seen as inappropriate or indiscreet. Some women mentioned that they got disapproving looks from strangers. For the women that were comfortable breastfeeding in public there was a confidence that they were doing nothing wrong, though few of them were even aware that laws protecting the right to breastfeed existed in their state. For example, Celeste said, "It's a fairly natural thing. Like I said, my take on it was if someone had a problem with it, that was their issue, not mine. I knew I wasn't doing anything wrong or anything illegal or anything offensive. I just went ahead and fed my baby." While confident in breastfeeding, she too gave attention to discretion. She explained, "I just had the standard old blanket. I kind of felt like hey, this is better than a screaming baby. You know what I mean?"

I found that even among women who breastfed extensively, there was a tendency to use terminology associated with indecent exposure. For example Christine said, "I don't know if I would have whipped it out in front of a male colleague or something, but I guess I just didn't and I don't think I would breastfeed in front of my students." When I asked Heather if she felt she had to give attention to being discreet, she said, "Oh yes. I wouldn't just whip it out. Thank you for saying that. I wouldn't just whip it out and expose myself. I was discreet." On parenting message boards, this is a common term that has come to be used to describe nursing in public, even among breastfeeding supporters.

Cathy, who told me she was never very comfortable breastfeeding in public, contrasted herself with her cousin saying, "I think it is personality. For me, I was more self-conscious. My cousin, when she's nursing . . . she couldn't care less. She would just whip it out and I remember being, 'Oh my gosh!'" Cathy humorously contrasted her own approach, "Even if I would do it, I would be so . . . I had to have the blankets. He'd be sweating." Another woman, Chaney who went back to work full-time six-weeks after the birth of each child said, "I always just had a blanket over me." Like Cathy, she stated she never felt comfortable breastfeeding in public. She continued, "Yeah, and if I had company over I would always go to a different room."

Kristine, who was exclusively breastfeeding her nine month-old stated:

> I think, like the breastfeeding in public, La Leche League's very much, this is good, you should be able to feel comfortable breastfeeding in public because it's completely natural. That's awesome and I agree as a concept, but I'm not ready to go out and lift my shirt up.

Kristine was involved in LLL and agreed with the group's principles to a very large extent. What she found challenging was that the culture in her area was not supportive of public breastfeeding; she did not see other people doing it, and this made it very difficult for her. She explained,

> We did it once at the airport and I was so proud of myself. We tend to time it that we go out and then we come back and she feeds and then naps. We tend not to be out when she needs to. If we do end up out when she needs to we tend to feed in the car. I have my emergency pillows in the car; I can move them round. It's partially just ease and partially just . . . especially in this area, I've never seen anyone breastfeeding around here. It's sad. It's terrible.

Though Kristine was a big supporter of LLL, she felt the organization sometimes failed to give enough attention to the problem of public breastfeeding being uncomfortable for many people. This is where she felt that the Kelly-Mom.com website had been more helpful to her than LLL for this particular issue. She elaborated,

> They kind of dismiss it. I think they tend to dismiss it because they want to
> downplay it like it's not a problem because they want you to breastfeed, which
> I get, but many of us really do have this uncomfortable feeling. She [Kelly
> Mom] can give you some more specific ways to do it.

Kristine also reported that even family members were uncomfortable when
she breastfed in front of them, even in her own home; she was not alone in
my sample of women. She explained to me:

> Even my brother, bless his heart; my brother is the most open-minded kid on
> the face of the planet, but even he was . . . he's trying to be cool about it. He's
> 30 now. He was kind of like, Oop, oop, there's a boob there. I was talking to
> him about the fact that isn't it sad that they're sexualized instead of being seen
> as big bottles. It's milk and that is their primary function; physiologically, they
> were made not for men, but for babies. Even he is having trouble. I think it is
> partially, until you have a child and you see how nonsexual and special this
> relationship is, it is hard because you've got this culturally preprogrammed
> sense that this region is just for men.

This comment represents what so many women related to me: breastfeeding was not sexual, but that public breastfeeding created discomfort because
of the sexualization of the breast in U.S. culture. For some women, like
Kristine, this caused them to stay home and avoid the issue as much as
possible.

I asked Chaney to explain why she was uncomfortable breastfeeding in
front of others and she had this to say:

> It was also just I didn't want to be stressed out about, worried about someone
> seeing me. I felt more comfortable in private and just the whole process went
> easier when I was just in a quiet room by myself with the baby. Yeah. I think
> I'm a little bit more of a private person in general that . . . I think there's still a
> thought of . . . there's such a divide between breast as a sexual object and
> breast as a functional object. I think because it is still, in my mind, viewed as a
> sexual object too that is meant to be seen by only people that you're intimate
> with, is more why I think I'm more uncomfortable with it and I'm just a more
> private person in general . . . Even though it's just there to feed the baby.

When I heard from Kristine again, she informed me that she was still
nursing her daughter who was now twenty-two months-old. She happily
reported that she was much more comfortable breastfeeding in public than
she was at the time of our interview. Ironically, she explained that she felt
more comfortable around strangers than family members and friends. She
said she had overcome many of her fears about public breastfeeding while
traveling in places where she knew no one.

A few of the women I spoke with were also LLL volunteers or lactation
consultants who had recently or were still nursing their own children. These

women had somewhat of a different take on public breastfeeding, in that they saw the very act of breastfeeding in public as a way of bringing about change in society. Like the other women, they recognized that nursing in public was not always commonly seen in some areas of the United States and argued that the more women do it, the less it will cause controversy.

For example, Erin F., who was training to be a LLL leader, said, "With my first baby, I remember being uncomfortable for a while, but it got better each time to the point where it doesn't even faze me anymore." She went on to state, "I feel the more I nurse in public, the better it is for women who are on the fence." She gave an example of how she felt that her own practice of breastfeeding in public helped other women. She explained:

> Yeah. I don't know; I feel that we have a responsibility . . . I remember the perfect example is that when my second daughter was born, I used to take my older daughter to story time at the library every week. I had never seen a woman nurse. I had seen them leave to nurse or bring a bottle, and so when my next one was born, we were in story time and I nursed her. The next week two moms nursed during the story time. Yeah. It takes somebody to break the ice.

She also spoke of trying to change a culture that is not supportive of caregivers in general:

> We just live in this culture where we think everything has to be done by ourselves and it's very hard to mother completely alone. You need a community of support whether it's for you or your children or advice . . . we're told when you drive up to your house, you drive in, you close your garage door, you get out of your car. You never see anyone. You lock your doors; you close your blinds, and then you can nurse as long as no one is over.

Julie Clark, a LLL leader and lactation consultant, had this to say:

> Basically because I really think it's completely grassroots, but every single time I go outside, whether I go to the grocery store, or I don't know, anywhere I go and I see a woman breastfeeding, I go to her and I give her positive reinforcement. Just someone to come over and say, "I'm really happy that you're doing this. Thank you. Because it makes my world easier too because I breastfeed."

Among those active in breastfeeding advocacy, there was more intentionality around normalizing breastfeeding and making it more comfortable for other women, though the idea that there is a need for support from other women was common among many of the women I interviewed. For example, Julie Carlton, who did not work outside the home when she was nursing, told me:

> I had a lot of girlfriends at the time and we would ask each other questions, you know, that kind of thing. We would have play groups where two moms would stay with all of the children while the other two moms would go out to lunch. Then, we would switch. It was a great support system that we created. I guess I surrounded myself with people like me. We needed to have that connection because, oh Lord. We all had the same philosophy. We would sit in the park and we would all be nursing.

Julie Carlton describes the support she felt from others who were also breastfeeding in her social circle. Many of the other women I spoke with found support among friends as well. Kristine, however, felt isolated as no one she knew breastfed, and she did not see it being done in public in her area. This prompted her to join LLL in order to seek out support; she eventually gained the courage to breastfeed in public.

Overall I found three groups of women: those who were fairly comfortable breastfeeding in public whenever it was necessary, those who avoided feeding in public due to discomfort with it, and a few who felt like they had a responsibility to nurse in public in order to pave the way for others and produce a more accepting culture. None of the women had been involved in conflicts over the practice or had participated in any nurse-ins. Many were unaware of state laws protecting public breastfeeding.

Support or Pressure From Others

Some of the women expressed that they had many like-minded friends who gave them a sense of support in what they were doing, while others did experience some pressure about their decisions about feeding. For example, Danielle, a nurse who worked part-time after a twelve-week maternity leave, had this to say when I asked if she felt any pressure from others; "No, but I move in a world where almost everyone breastfeeds. No. I never came across that. Most of my friends stayed home, so I don't know. My best friend, she breastfed twins, she breasted all of them. I don't know, I lived in this little bubble."

She did go on to say that as her daughter got older, she would get some comments. She explained:

> Not initially, but when she got older random comments would be made but I can't remember what they were and they didn't really do much. I didn't feel pressure to stop. But um, I would get, 'you're still breastfeeding?' I would just say, 'Yes.' I didn't get, it wasn't intense; it was just you know . . . were people surprised? Maybe, and I was different. I parented differently than all of my sisters and all of my cousins. So, I am not sure, they were probably just like that's just Danielle. It was my sisters and my cousins, but really, never my friends.

Erin D., who primarily used formula with her six children, said that she did not get pressure from her friends that were breastfeeding, but she did get some from her family. She explained:

> My sister is a big proponent of breastfeeding so I got a lot of it from her. She is also a nurse. Oh yeah. My family was like, 'Why won't you breastfeed? Well you didn't give it enough time. You have to give it time. So, are you going to breastfeed this time? You have to just push through it.' I got it with all of them, every time. 'So, are you going to breastfeed this time?' That was the first question. 'So, you're going to breastfeed this time, right?'

On the other hand, Kristine said that before going to LLL, she did not know anyone else who was breastfeeding and that it made her feel "like a rebel." She said, "I really like the idea of nursing until she decides she's no longer interested." However, she said she felt the reaction from others was negative. She explained that from her perspective, the message was, "It's great that you're breastfeeding, and when are you stopping?" To illustrate this further she told me, "Somebody said to me, 'Well, if the child is able to unbutton your shirt, they're probably a little too old.' It's like. 'Really?'"

This suggests the importance of groups like LLL for those who may not already have a group of similarly-situated friends. LLL leaders, Erin F. and Julie Clark both explained that they felt they owed it to other women to express their support and help pave the way for them by going against the broader culture to do what they felt was best.

Experiences with Health Care Providers

Several women in my sample felt their pediatricians were not as supportive of breastfeeding as they had anticipated, given how highly it is recommended by the AAP. Two issues came up in the interviews: weight and sleep. For example, Celeste explained to me why she changed pediatricians:

> She actually said I was nursing him too much and that I needed to find another way to pacify him. Grant was a big baby. I found another pediatrician and he said, 'You're fine. You are not over-feeding him. He's not spitting up; he doesn't have reflux. He's a baby. Babies are chubby. It's no big deal. Don't worry about it.'

Celeste's new pediatrician was supportive of breastfeeding, not just to meet nutritional needs but to meet comfort needs as well. For example, she explained that after his infant patients received injections, he gave mothers time to nurse if they wished to calm their babies down. Celeste simply handled her conflicts by finding a pediatrician who was more like-minded about breastfeeding and how it should be done.

While weight was a common theme in the women's stories about conflicts with pediatricians, most cases involved the babies not gaining enough
weight, rather than too much. Christine explained that her son had some
problems latching on and that she did a lot of pumping in the first six weeks.
She said, "He was losing weight and he was a month old and still losing.
They tried to . . . but I did not want to supplement with formula." She
pumped and fed him her milk in a bottle until the problems resolved and he
was able to latch on without a problem. He fed at the breast until he was
about thirteen months old.

In Amey's case, she reported to me that her health care providers were
supportive overall but that two of her younger five biological children were
not gaining weight well:

> They weren't gaining weight as much and part of that for me was because . . .
> and our pediatrician was a friend of mine from college so he could talk very
> frankly with me. He said this happens to people who have a lot of kids because
> you're so busy. Yeah. You're just not thinking about it. Because it is true. I
> was buzzing around this place. And he said they won't eat as much and they
> sleep more and they're not causing you problems, so you forget about nursing
> them. But he was very active about, 'Set your timer, get up in the middle of the
> night, yada, yada, yada . . .'

Then, as problems continued, Amey explained that the doctor's advice
changed. She said,

> Yeah, but when she was about a month old and she still wasn't gaining, he
> said, 'You need to put her on formula.' He said, 'Till you can get her to
> gaining a little bit more, get her on formula for a little bit.' But that first month
> he was really willing to . . .

Amey chose to simply nurse her daughter more frequently and not to supplement her with formula. This solved the problem and her daughter began to
gain weight. In this way, Amey was able to respond to the weight gain issue
in a manner she saw appropriate without any direct conflict with her doctor.
This was similar to Christine's response to advice to supplement her son. She
found her own solution to her son's slow weight gain by pumping and feeding her son who had difficulty latching onto the breast.

Like Celeste, Kristine ended up changing pediatricians over differences
of philosophy having to do with infant feeding. She explained:

> Honestly, our biggest problem was not our experience or our belief in breast-
> feeding or any of that; it was our pediatrician. We thought we had the perfect
> doctors. Very quickly it was 'well, you can start mixing rice cereal and stuff
> with the milk.' This was at three or four months, they were already starting to
> suggest it.

Some of the doctor's recommendations seemed to be connected to expectations about infants and sleep. Kristine explained how the doctor said, "Well, she should still be going through the night. She's in your room; you really need to move her to another room so that she learns to sleep through the night."

Kristine felt her daughter's doctors paid a great deal of lip service to breastfeeding, but then made suggestions that conflicted with what she saw as typical behavior for breastfed babies. She stated, "They said they supported breastfeeding, but all their recommendations were very much things that kill your supply and your ability to do it." On its face, the rice cereal mixed with milk suggestion presupposes either formula or pumped milk when the AAP recommendation is six months of exclusive breastfeeding. Kristine explained the way she handled the conflict:

> We realized that we needed to make a change in the pediatrician. I can see how other mothers going would have a totally different experience and say, 'wait a second, the doctor is telling me I need to have her sleeping through the night regardless of what it does to my milk supply.'

While Kristine was able to solve her conflict by changing doctors, she recognized the effect this approach could have on breastfeeding practices, given that her health providers were part of one of the most highly-ranked pediatric practices in the area.

While most women I interviewed did not report disagreements over infant feeding with their pediatricians, those that did either followed their own judgment, despite the doctor's advice, or they switched pediatricians in cases of major conflict.

Several women reported that their infants were given formula in the hospital for various reasons, even though they were breastfeeding. Cathy said,

> He was in the NIC unit right away. We had problems with his liver . . . I had a really high fever. My heart rate was down. They were taking care of me . . . Actually, his first feeding was formula. They knew I wanted to breastfeed. I guess they needed to feed him. It was one of those things. I didn't even really know. It was a weird thing. I felt, 'oh my gosh! Is this going to be okay?'

Also, Julie Carlton reported,

> I do remember saying to them, no don't give her formula because I want to be able to nurse; and I remember them pressuring me; they said, 'She's hungry.' I did supplement because I felt pressure. I was nervous and tense and thought, 'Oh my God . . . my baby's starving.' That was their solution. They pushed formula because they didn't want to deal with her crying.

She explained that the hospital was very full with many women having babies that particular weekend, and that she barely got a room. A few months later, she discovered a dairy intolerance was causing her baby's frequent crying; she had success with cutting dairy out of her diet.

On the other hand, Erin D., who experienced problems breastfeeding her first child, reported pressure to breastfeed from one of the nurses at the hospital with her first birth, but not with her other children whom she fed formula from the beginning. She described what happened in the hospital:

> Yeah. This one nurse kept bringing breast pumps in and saying you really need to pump; you at least should pump. This nurse was very pushy about it. I didn't like her. I finally, like the third or fourth time she brought the pump in, I said, 'I'm not interested. Take it out of my room.'

Julie Carlton also reported an unpleasant experience, which she thought may have been related to the crowded conditions in the hospital when she gave birth. She said,

> I was so tense in the hospital. I wanted the lactation consultant to teach me how to do it properly. She was so rude. She was so forceful, so mean, and she talked so fast and you know this is what you should do . . . boom, boom, boom. I was picturing someone who was going to take time and show me and every-thing. Yeah. Not at all.

Not all the women I spoke with had conflicts with medical professionals while they were breastfeeding. Those that did have conflicts found ways to cope with the situation as best they could. Some changed physicians, while others just did what they thought was best to solve the problem, without challenging the doctors directly.

Views on Breastfeeding Advocacy and Feminism

I found that even among those women who exclusively fed breast milk in the first year, there were differences of opinion on how much government and non-profit advocacy for breastfeeding was appropriate. Some women ex-pressed their views in terms of feminism, while others did not. For example, Christine, who worked full-time and pumped milk for her boys, showed concern about too much pressure to breastfeed:

> There is this chapter in the book produced by La Leche League, *The Womanly Art of Breastfeeding*. There is a whole chapter; they basically discourage you from returning to work and they cite these studies . . . And I was like that's it, forget this La Leche League; if I have any issues with breastfeeding, I am going to go somewhere else because it was basically you are a terrible mother and your kid will be a serial killer because studies show that children who

don't spend enough time with the mother figure end up being detached from people.

She added her thoughts on breastfeeding as a feminist issue:

> I think that is why it's such a, why some people would say, oh it's not a feminist issue because some people, it's tied to our biology and for me when I read that I was so offended and it turned me off of this entire group, and its so funny because my son is the most affectionate and so sweet with his brother and you know I went back to work with him when he was six weeks old. . . . They cited one sociologist and you know you're already kind of feeling torn as it is, but it's basically you know, I mean what they didn't allow for is that some people will have to go back to work. They will have to work full time.

Christine's uneasiness with breastfeeding as a feminist issue is linked to LLL and its history of discouraging mothers of young children from working (LLL 2004). While the organization has shifted its approach to this issue in more recent years (LLL 2010), many feminist scholars have expressed a similar concern—while LLL values mothering, it also essentializes women as primarily mothers by emphasizing the young child's need for "all of her" (Blum 1999; Bobel 2001; LLL 2004).

None of the other women expressed specific objections to breastfeeding as a feminist issue, but most had not considered it one way or the other. However, Cathy, who worked part-time and nursed her son for about fourteen months, separated the issue of pressure to breastfeed from the right to breastfeed. She said,

> I think it would definitely come under women's rights. If I choose not to breastfeed or if I never have a child, I still want to support those women who should be able to go anywhere they want. If you want to, you should be able to have every support you can get; if you choose not to, you shouldn't feel ashamed.

Christine, on the other hand, saw these issues as more interconnected than Cathy did. Christine explained how she felt too much support for breastfeeding women could make other women feel pressured to breastfeed. She told me,

> I would see things on Facebook that we need to advocate for private places where someone can pump at work; and I'm like, yeah, that's fine but at the same time if somebody makes that choice that they don't want to do it, then you know what I mean? I felt a little bit uncomfortable with it. I know I was lucky because I have a private place to pump. It's kind of a fine line because I have mixed feelings about how much to defend the whole right to breastfeed because I feel like when you do this, it is kind of putting pressure on somebody to breastfeed in a way, too.

Most of the women I spoke with opposed pressuring women to breastfeed. Most saw breastfeeding as a choice, but many felt providing pumping support and protecting the right to breastfeed in public did not constitute a lack of support for those who choose not to breastfeed. In fact, Cathy saw supporting breastfeeding rights as something all women should support because it defends a woman's right to make decisions about her body. I think perhaps the issues get linked because breastfeeding advocacy often takes an approach that focuses on changing individual behavior without also focusing on broader structural influences and barriers. Since some women link the issue of breastfeeding rights to breastfeeding advocacy they may hesitate to support it, even if they breastfeed themselves.

Kristine, who left her government job at Homeland Security to stay home with her daughter in her early years, felt breastfeeding rights could be seen as a feminist issue, but she explained why she had not tended to see it that way until more recently. She explained that when she left work, she felt that most feminists would see that as a very non-feminist thing to do. She put it this way:

> I almost felt like it was the opposite of the women's rights because it's so focused on . . . it's so hard to do while working. I associate so much of the women's rights movement as related to my right-to-work and so I guess I always saw it as almost the opposite. Feminists go back to work and those of us who are choosing a different path somehow are not living up to that historical legacy. My mom was very much part of that movement.

Kristine was very much a supporter of a woman's right to work outside the home, or not work outside the home. She felt the women's movement really had not focused on the latter. She went on to explain:

> Our right to work is there now. It may not be perfect, but that part is taken care of. What we really need is actually our right to not work, our right to work partially, our right to be moms is where we actually are most lacking right now . . . I feel like to some degree, my perception of feminism is, at least the way that it was portrayed to me growing up, it was all about telling us that we could have it all. Then there's the reality that we can't have it all. There are compromises no matter what. There's only twenty-four hours in a day. There's only so many ways you can split that time. The new feminism almost has to be the flexible version of whatever. You having the right to choose your version of that balance. If that involves breastfeeding, then that's perfectly okay. It's funny because I never associated it with feminism at all, which is sad; it should be an inherent part of it.

Kristine points out a general lack of support for mothers and mothering, and her perception that the women's movement has not really been focused on supporting motherhood in the United States. She also critiques the way breastfeeding advocacy has focused too much on the individual woman and not enough on the ways society is structured that are not conducive to breast-feeding.

Kristine had this to say about breastfeeding advocacy more generally:

> I wish that we could all focus less on what everyone is doing and more on why they're doing it. If they're giving a bottle because there is a medical reason, focus on why, if they're doing a bottle because they didn't get the support for breastfeeding, then you shouldn't hate them for using a bottle, we should feel sad that we as a culture didn't make them feel supported enough. If I end up not breastfeeding past a few weeks, why was that? If it was because I didn't get the support I needed, that's a sad thing. It's not about the mother's failure; it's about society's failure.

Kristine raises many issues in her comments that go beyond educating women about breastfeeding. She frames the issue in a way that corresponds to the critique many feminist scholars make of an approach where women are individually held responsible for the care and well-being of society's citizens, where the responsibility for providing the best possible care is placed solely on the women rather than on the society as a whole (Law 2000; Tronto 2013; Wolf 2011; Woliver 2002). Rather than opposing breastfeeding advocacy altogether because of this problem, she suggests a focus on providing real support and educating the public and employers on breastfeeding.

Attitudes Toward Others' Infant Feeding Practices

Kristine's suggestions for not focusing on what other women are doing, but why they are doing it illustrates a theme of non-judgment I found among the women I interviewed. I really failed to find a mommy wars mentality; most women felt that their decisions were the right ones for themselves and their families, but they refrained from judging others. For example, Heather, who breastfed four children said, "I try not to judge people. If I see somebody bottle feeding, I figure that there's a reason why they're not breastfeeding. It's always nice and beautiful to see a child being breastfed, but I never assume, 'Oh, they're horrible mothers because they're not breastfeeding.' They have their reason, whatever it may be."

Another illustration of an absence of mommy wars thinking came from mother of six, Erin D., who had problems breastfeeding her first child and used formula exclusively with each child after that. For example, she failed to see why there should be a controversy about breastfeeding in the public space. She explained,

> I can just speak for me. If I see somebody breastfeeding in public, I look away. If I don't want to see it, I don't have to see it. I look away not because it makes

me uncomfortable, but because I don't think people want to be stared at, you know and I don't think that's why people are breastfeeding in public. You know, it's not like, 'hey look at me.' It's because their kid is hungry and it's a natural way of feeding.

In general, the women in my sample felt breastfeeding was natural, yet at the same time, they did not presume to know what it was like for others. They recognized that women used formula for a variety of reasons, and refrained from passing judgment.

Use of Risk Language in Breastfeeding Advocacy

I asked women about their reactions to various approaches to breastfeeding advocacy. Most were familiar with the approach often called *Breast is Best*. It discusses the health benefits of breastfeeding by referring to lower incidence of various health problems for breastfed infants as compared to infants fed formula. On the other hand, the risk approach (which is discussed at length in chapter 5) involves advocacy that couches formula feeding as a practice that increases the risk of disease, as is done in anti-smoking health messaging. Not smoking is the default biological norm; smoking is deviation from that norm that increases health risk. In this approach, breastfeeding is used as the default or baseline from which to judge health outcomes (Wiessinger 2001).

This approach was taken in the Health and Human Services and Ad Council, National Breastfeeding Awareness Campaign of 2004-2006. Television ads run during this campaign featured very pregnant women riding mechanical bulls in bars and engaging in a logrolling contest. The implication was: since women would not take these kinds of risks while pregnant, they should not expose their infants to the risks of greater incidence of disease by using formula to feed them after they are born. The ads have been posted on You Tube by BabyAmyRose2010 and were still available as of this writing. Most of the women I interviewed had never seen the ads, but I described them, as well as comparisons of formula use and smoking that have been used by those advocating this approach (Wiessinger 2001).

While most of the women I interviewed felt positively about breastfeeding advocacy in general, when I asked women for their perspectives on the risks of formula approach to breastfeeding advocacy, only one felt this was a good approach; another thought it might be okay. Michele said, "I think the wording that they're trying to change to is appropriate, I mean you are deciding to bring a life into the world; so with that decision you need to know what is best for them." When I asked Heather if she felt this approach was okay, she replied, "In a way. I guess I can see how it would sound a little harsh comparing it to smoking, but my opinion is if you can breastfeed, breastfeed and if you can't, formula is okay."

In contrast, the others, while they frequently mentioned the health benefits of breastfeeding as a reason they breastfed, expressed a great deal of
concern over the use of the *risk approach* to advocacy in the United States.
Kristine had this to say:

> Couple thoughts. First, I don't think all the advertising should be focused on
> the woman. Going back to the whole guilt and everything else; instead of
> saying, 'Why would you take those risks with your baby?' focus more on
> why . . . why people don't breastfeed rarely has to do with not loving or caring
> about their baby. It's all about lack of awareness, lack of ability, lack of feeling
> comfortable. Making them feel guilty is not going to change those things.

She did not deny that there were risks or that people should be informed, but
felt this approach was not helpful because it did not do anything to address
the constraints that may keep many women from breastfeeding. When I
asked her to elaborate, she continued:

> If they truly think that the lack of awareness of the benefits or the risks is the
> totality of the story, then I guess . . . I feel like it's missing the mark on why
> people don't do it, and making them feel guilty is not going to make them
> better mothers. I would wish they would focus more on the larger societal
> issues. HHS has an incredible platform from which they can advocate for a
> public breastfeeding day or whatever. Why isn't HHS doing training programs
> for companies and developing training modules that all companies could use?
> Focus on the men; focus on the society, focus on the employers.

While this particular mother gave the most detailed response to the risk
approach, many others had similar concerns.

For the most part, the women did not think the use of the term *risky* for
formula made sense. They knew all about the medical evidence, but continued to think of this as the benefits of breastfeeding, or breastfeeding lowering
risks, rather than formula increasing risk. They mostly associated the word
risks with life or death situations, and did not tend to see the medical evidence in this way. For example, when I asked about the idea of formula as
putting infants at risk in a way similar to smoking, Erin D. said,

> Oh no uh-uh. That makes me mad. That's stupid. That is not the same thing. It
> is not putting a chemical into someone's body. They make formula to be as
> close to breast milk as possible. It's not like you are pumping rat poison or
> arsenic or whatever into your baby's system. I do think that breastfeeding
> is . . . It is the most natural, closest to nature. I mean it is the most natural and
> the way our bodies were designed. But if your body does not function the way
> it was designed and you have to go to another way, I don't think that should be
> a big deal. You shouldn't be made to feel like a second-class citizen.

Erin D.'s response is interesting because, though she used more formula than other women in the study, she had a reaction that was not much different than most of the others I spoke with. In fact, she emphasized the naturalness of breastfeeding while also rejecting the risk language, even though formula ended up working out best in her situation.

This was a common viewpoint among the women I interviewed, ranging from those who mostly used formula to those who exclusively or primarily breastfed well beyond the first or second year. For example, Amey, who breastfed all five of her biological children for one to three years each, worked part-time, and fed an adopted child formula, had this to say about the HHS NBAC ad campaign:

> Wow. When you talked about this ad, first of all, I do not think it is a good analogy. I do not say nine months pregnant riding a rodeo bull in a bar is even comparable to deciding you are going to formula-feed your kid; that is so far removed. That is not even a good analogy; it is not even comparable.

Amey did recognize some risks to formula use, saying, "To me formula-feeding a baby, it has some risks, obviously. Absolutely allergy. I knew about them because I read about them, and that was a reason I wanted to breastfeed."

When I asked why she felt so strongly against the risk approach taken by the ads even though she saw some risks to formula use, she replied, "I think it is too guilt-inducing. It is too much. There is enough guilt. You want to inform people and that was enough to motivate me. But I think all this business about you are causing harm to your child, we get enough of that as a parent." She also mentioned something that many feminists have pointed out when she stated, "It looks like you are saying, 'You are a bad person because you are not breastfeeding.'" Like Kristine, she talked about more substantive ways that breastfeeding could be supported. She explained:

> If they want to increase this, they need to do something about maternity leaves. I cannot imagine doing it if I did not have that six-month maternity leave. The number one thing they could do, from my perspective, would be allow for longer maternity leaves. I cannot imagine that they would necessarily be paid because we do not have the tax system in place to support paid maternity leave, but even just the option.

While Amey had been allowed to take unpaid leave for six months with her first child and nine months with the others, she recognized this as an obstacle for many people she knew:

> Right, I was lucky to have the option to even ask for an unpaid leave; a lot of people would ask for unpaid and it would be no. I know people like you who they purposely set . . . up their lives so that they have the option of, "I am

going to teach this class now, I can run home and nurse . . . and I am going to teach this class now and run home and nurse." If you are working an 8:00 to 5:00 factory job, you do not have that option.

Amey's conclusion that the ads would produce guilt rather than doing anything to support women was typical of the responses I received when I talked with women about the risk approach to breastfeeding advocacy. Overall, women suggested a variety of alternative approaches ranging from educating employers and the public to longer family leaves. While only one felt the approach was definitely appropriate and one thought it might be, they both also recognized barriers that women face to successful breastfeeding and that formula may be necessary in some cases.

In keeping with the risk approach, some breastfeeding advocates have suggested that formula only be made available by prescription. None of the women I interviewed took this position, but some who were also breastfeeding advocates had considered it in the past. Most just felt it was unrealistic, even if they were big proponents of breastfeeding. One breastfeeding advocate who had nursed four children explained,

> Well, no . . . I don't want to ban formula. I did, for a while, think that formula should only be available by prescription; but I was convinced that it would then become a class issue. Women would have to make a doctor's appointment and have additional health care costs to get prescriptions.

Danielle said this about requiring a prescription,

> My issue is that you have to fix other problems first in order to make that work . . . You have to put things into place so if you want that woman to breastfeed for a year, she either won't have to go back to work for a year, or you have to set it up so that she has more resources. You have got to do something; otherwise it is not realistic. So what's going to happen if formula can only be by prescription, so you are going to have a black market for formula? People will do it, ya know. There is a black market for everything else, for Pete's sake; you are going have a black market for formula, which is ridiculous.

When asked about her reaction to the risk language, she had this to say,

> There are risks to just about everything . . . it's too much pressure and it should be that you try to make the formula healthier, I don't know. We are so caught up on this whole thing for this one year of breastfeeding, but what about the five years that you are feeding your children crap?

Danielle attempts to put risk in perspective. Similarly, Law (2000) has pointed out that parents are constantly weighing a wide variety of risks and benefits for their families, making the best decision they can under the constraints they face. While many women recognized barriers to breastfeeding and the need for people to make decisions based on their families needs, most also saw the need for supportive policies and approaches to advocacy.

Challenges to Breastfeeding

Most women I talked to felt that the biggest reason that many women don't breastfeed as long as the AAP recommends was due to returning to work. Michele, who left work outside the home after giving birth to her first child, had this to say:

> I think it is work. I can't imagine. I mean, I would push through it because, you know, that's my personality, but I can't imagine going back to work and dealing with what I had dealt with, you know. I can't imagine that. I mean, I would do it I think. Yeah. But, um, I can see why it happens.

The women I spoke with repeatedly said that they were fortunate when they were able to breastfeed, stay home with their children, take leave, or have facilities to pump. These did not appear to be things they thought everyone had access to and therefore, they reserved judgment on others with different situations. While my sample was comprised mostly of middle-class women with a variety of working and feeding situations, they all seemed to recognize that they were privileged in ways that others were not. For example Amey told me:

> I can't imagine not doing it . . . if everything's fine. But I also very quickly say, "It's not right for everybody." You have to make the decision that works for you. It worked for me. I was fortunate I had all these healthy babies. Everybody has to do their own research.

While Amey was a strong supporter of breastfeeding, she recognized differences among individual circumstances and the need for people to do what works best for them. Regardless of their own situations, the women tended to see work as a potential challenge and were sympathetic to the challenges others may face when combining breastfeeding and working.

Several women I spoke with pumped milk for their babies while they worked full- or part-time; a few also nursed their children either by going to their children at lunch or having them brought to them during breaks. While working did not prevent them from breastfeeding, they talked about some of the challenges of combining these activities.

Christine, who returned to work after six weeks and nursed her first son for thirteen months and her second son for ten months, said when she weaned her youngest son a bit earlier than she had planned, "I cannot try and squeeze the time in to pump and be running on no sleep. I was just so tired." While she had worked and pumped for many months with both her sons successfully, she talked about her youngest son's desire to nurse all night when she had to work and pump the next day, and the toll it took on her. "To be honest, I got to the point where he was ten months and he still was not sleeping, and I was just like, you know, because he constantly wanted it and it was like, I just can't do this."

Christine explained what pumping was like at work:

> It would be about two or three times at work. That I think was the hardest part because it's basically like constantly you're stealing away and someone's always going to be knocking on the door or people will be calling you. You keep, you can't really do something else; you can maybe read an email but it's not like you can really focus on doing something else when the thing is going. I found it very distracting.

Danielle returned to work one day a week after a twelve-week leave. She explained, "I pumped at work twice. I pumped at lunch and then I pumped at another break. I tried to work sometimes but I couldn't always. Sometimes I would try to do phone calls while I was pumping but it didn't always work." Chaney returned to work full-time at six weeks and pumped at work. Like Christine, she had a fairly conducive work environment but also explained that even in a good situation, finding total privacy in the workplace could be a bit tricky. She explained:

> I had a little sign on the door that said, 'Privacy, please do not enter.' People would still try to open the door and it would scare me. I knew it was always locked but it was like . . . and then you'd relax again. Do you know what I mean? They'd still try the door even though it's like, 'You do not want to walk in on this.'

While pumping worked fairly well for these women, their stories illustrate what they experienced and how it could be difficult to remove themselves from the work environment to have real privacy, even when they had a locked place to go since coworkers would continue to look for them or seek access to the rooms they were in.

Cathy, who worked part-time while she was breastfeeding, described how her husband brought her son to her at work to nurse. She had gotten approval from her supervisor, and no one ever told her she couldn't nurse at work in her office, but she sometimes felt disapproval. She explained, "There was one woman. She never said anything. I just remember . . . sixth sense that they think 'really?'"

Amey worked part-time after taking a six-month leave with her first son and talked about how she was able to make nursing on her lunch hour work because her son's day care was close by and her husband also worked with her. Prior to that, she had tried pumping but there was no good private place to pump. She explained, "There was a bathroom there, but you'd have to sit on the toilet. A public toilet doesn't have a cover to sit on. So, you're standing in the stall, trying to pump, dressed in a dress that isn't necessarily a nursing friendly dress." She explained how she found another solution:

> He was at daycare. For his first three years, he was in a daycare and I drove there and I nursed him at lunchtime. I remember eating lunch on the way there and then I would nurse him at lunch; and I think Lloyd may have eaten lunch while I was nursing because he drove there while I was eating lunch.

She explained that her son was eating rice cereal and drinking juice at this point, so she only did the lunch routine for about a month and then nursed him before and after work after that without using formula.

The stories of combining work and breastfeeding illustrate some of the challenges faced by the women I interviewed. In my sample, only one woman, Christine, had breastfed and pumped while working full-time for an entire year with her first son. Even those with a private place that could be locked and was not a bathroom experienced some anxiety due to coworkers knocking on the door, and not being able to really get any work done while pumping. The women's experiences showed the difficulty of combining breastfeeding and working in the current workplace environment. No one I interviewed had a paid leave of more than six weeks.

Other Challenges

I discovered that while some women had a difficult time meeting breastfeeding goals they had set for themselves, others ended up nursing longer than they had planned. Chaney expressed that she wanted to breastfeed because of the health benefits she had read about; but since she had a breast reduction she was not sure if and how much she would be able to breastfeed. She said, "I was going to give it a go and go from there." She nursed her first son for six weeks and her second son for about three months, but also supplemented with formula. She had originally planned on trying to breastfeed for about six months. She explained that she did not have any issues with latching or with switching between bottle and breast. When I asked about any challenges she faced, she said, "It was keeping up with the demand . . . It was that and it was frustration on my part. I knew he was still hungry. Do you know what I mean?"

Other women in my sample spoke about the feeling that they were not producing enough milk. For example, Julie Carlton, who nursed both of her girls—two years apart in age—explained it this way:

My goal was a year. Just from reading. I didn't make it either. Both of them went through a growth spurt and both of them were requiring more and my body wasn't producing more at the rate that they wanted it, and I'm sure it would have if I was persistent, but then I started to worry. . . . They seemed hungrier. I knew when my breast milk was gone but they wouldn't pop off.

Both girls were weaned by ten and nine months respectively. Because Julie had challenges with pumping, she expressed some frustration with not being able to go places without her children. She said,

You know from my experience, probably by six months I wanted to go out for a longer period of time and get my life back, you know what I mean; and since I was having trouble with pumping, I was really tied to them. . . . It was starting to be a sacrifice in that . . . I still enjoyed it obviously but I could see how people would stop. I would like to go on a date with my husband, you know.

Cathy, on the hand, originally thought she might breastfeed for about four months but she ended up weaning at thirteen months. By that time, she actually wanted to continue nursing but had to stop when a serious dog bite required her to go on medication that the doctor said could not be taken while nursing. She explained, "Yes. It was more abrupt than I had planned. . . . It was so hard. It was harder for me than it was for him."

While women described their breastfeeding experiences as positive overall, many women experienced mixed feelings about it. For example, Christine told me:

Yeah. I mean on the one hand I loved it, at night being able to help him and giving him something that was mine, and it was mostly a good experience, but sometimes living by the three hours where you are constantly having to be. . . . I just felt very imprisoned by my biology.

While it was sometimes challenging for women to be the only one who was able to feed the baby, sometimes fathers were able to provide assistance by using a bottle of pumped breast milk or supplemental formula to feed their infants. This posed another kind of problem. For example, Christine explained to me:

I remember getting frustrated trying to figure out how to do everything and I was pumping and he said, 'Is there anything I can do?' And I said, 'Can you lactate?' And so it was kind of frustrating in that respect because my husband always wanted to throw a bottle at him and then I would have to pump.

In Chaney's case she felt some of her supply issues, especially with her first son, stemmed from her husband's desire to be involved in helping with feeding. She said,

> I think he wanted to be very involved in helping feed the boys when naturally he doesn't have breasts so he couldn't do that. If I didn't wake up, he would just go and fix the bottle instead of waking me up to say, 'You need to go feed the baby.' I think there were times where I could have had the opportunity to do it. . . . Whereas with my youngest son, I did a lot better job of getting up no matter what; and I would set my alarm even if he wasn't up. I was pumping just to make sure I was on a regular schedule.

Because Chaney was breastfeeding and using formula due to her breast reduction, this made it easy for her husband to help. But she also recognized how she had to be diligent about breastfeeding and pumping when she could in order to keep up her milk supply.

On the other hand, Erin D. found her husband's ability to help with bottle-feeding to be one of the major advantages to using formula. When I asked if her husband was supportive of her decision to switch to formula with her first son, she said, "I think he liked it because he got to do it too. I think he liked it, but not in the middle of the night. Nobody likes it in the middle of the night."

What Women's Stories Reveal

The stories presented here reflect some of the infant feeding joys and challenges women experience. While most of the women in my sample had been able to breastfeed for at least a few months, none of them passed judgment on other women. Rather, most of them felt that more support was needed in order for women to breastfeed longer, if they so desired. While the sample is not meant to be representative of all women, it shows how women view their own experiences and those of others around them. While they saw the choice to breastfeed or not as an individual decision, the need for social and professional support was not lost on them. Some women focused a great deal on maternity or family-leave policies, while others talked about support in the hospital, workplace pumping facilities, and creating more support for public breastfeeding or providing private facilities for breastfeeding women in public spaces.

Women in my sample stressed health benefits as a major reason for their decision to breastfeed. Also, many of the women, regardless of whether they mostly breastfed or mostly used formula, saw breastfeeding as natural. Linda Blum (1999) found that this feeling varied across demographic groups in her qualitative study of infant feeding. The fact that so many of the women in my sample had been breastfed themselves will also vary across groups. These are issues that need further exploration across racial, ethnic, and class groups. The view of breastfeeding as natural is similar to Blum's (1999) findings for this demographic group that primarily consisted of middle-class, married, white women across a variety of work situations. The fact that many were themselves breastfed is an avenue for further research as well. As breastfeeding rates increase, there could be an echo effect of women in the next generation breastfeeding because they or their siblings were breastfed. Since the increases in breastfeeding rates in the 1990s were primarily driven by increases in breastfeeding rates among less educated women and racial and ethnic minorities, an echo effect for these groups may be coming. Survey data could shed light on these trends, while further qualitative studies with varied groups of women can get at this dynamic in greater detail.

The fact that I found women, some committed to extended breastfeeding, who were very uncomfortable with breastfeeding in public, shows how difficult it can be for some women to challenge these cultural norms, even when they are highly committed to breastfeeding. While it would be hard to get data on how many women are prevented from breastfeeding at all due to this concern, it is definitely something to further investigate. Maclean (1990) found discomfort over breastfeeding in public to be a major reason women chose not to breastfeed in her study of Canadian women (27). Kristine's suggestion about educating the public about breastfeeding has been echoed by Kedrowski and Lipscomb (2008), who found somewhat limited support for public breastfeeding in their study of breastfeeding rights.

Most of the women I interviewed did not agree with the risk approach to breastfeeding advocacy. Most women I interviewed felt this approach would make women feel guilty for not breastfeeding when they may not be able to do so. Yet, if we take Kristine's approach and concentrate on addressing cultural constraints to breastfeeding, this could go a long way in providing women the opportunity to breastfeed without judging their parenting decisions.

While formula use ranged among the women in the sample, most of the women expressed that they did not feel they faced too much pressure not to use formula, if and when they decided to use it. One did experience this from family members, but not from breastfeeding friends. More women in my sample (perhaps because many did breastfeed for a few months or more) actually reported pressure to feed their children formula, either in the hospital or by pediatricians. This illustrates the paradox of enthusiastic advocacy for breastfeeding in a culture that still promotes or assumes formula use, often even within the medical community. Issues of slow weight gain seemed to bring advice from pediatricians to supplement with formula in a bottle or switch to formula entirely, rather than immediate referrals to a lactation consultant for professional evaluation and instruction on proper supplementation.

The respondents in my sample all seemed to recognize that they possessed class privilege as they spoke of how difficult breastfeeding would be in situations different from their own. It was common for breastfeeding women to describe themselves as lucky or blessed, especially if they chose to leave work to be a full-time parent. On the one hand, this kept them from judging others, and also prompted some of them to suggest maternity leaves and supportive workplace policies. On the other hand, most did not question the inequalities at the heart of these differences.

Most of the women I interviewed reported that their family and friends were generally supportive of their decisions about breastfeeding and formula use, although some preferred breastfeeding not be done in their presence. While some experienced disapproving comments, most felt comfortable that their decisions were best for their families and did not feel overly pressured to change their decisions. While my sample was composed primarily of married, white, middle-class women in a variety of employment situations, they still faced challenges and felt that cultural norms, workplace programs, and family leave policies could all contribute to removing challenges to breastfeeding.

Some paradoxical themes emerged from the analysis. On the one hand, most of the women in this particular sample saw breastfeeding as natural; but they also saw it as something they felt privileged to be able to do, especially if they were able to stay home with their infants while they were breastfeeding. The theme of choice ran through most of the narratives as well. Women reserved judgment of others since breastfeeding was a choice, and women faced varying situations. While it was refreshing not to see a *mommy wars* emerge, it felt a bit contradictory to describe breastfeeding as both the natural thing and a choice they felt privileged to be able to make. Perhaps, by seeing themselves as lucky or blessed, they recognized that while breastfeeding may be "a natural way to feed a baby," it is not always an easy thing to do in the U.S. cultural and workplace context. This is not a surprising response given the paradox of strong breastfeeding advocacy in the United States, simultaneously coupled with working and cultural conditions that can make breastfeeding difficult.

While many recognized that supportive workplace and public policies could help women breastfeed if they desired to do so, I found that only those few with connections to LLL and Attachment Parenting International spoke in terms of the need for fundamental changes in the structure of U.S. society that would value caregiving in a substantial way. These women saw the path to these changes as starting with their own actions of breastfeeding in public or practicing attachment parenting, but they also expressed support for family-leave policies and other practices that would support breastfeeding and parenting in general.

Those without involvement in one of these organizations tended to see circumstances that made it easier or harder to breastfeed as a given, and then go from there to make the best decisions for their families. In fact, they seemed to accept challenging conditions for breastfeeding as normal, and felt that they were lucky or privileged to be able to do it, either because they could afford to take time out of full-time employment or had jobs that could accommodate pumping or breastfeeding.

While most of those interviewed were in favor of providing more support for breastfeeding women, none were involved in explicitly political activism themselves. The activism of Erin F. and Julie Clark focuses on individual everyday actions and how they can change the culture when they spread and accumulate throughout a community. They felt the best way to make breastfeeding possible for others was to breastfeed anywhere and support others who were doing the same.

In terms of advocacy, most women felt that it was appropriate to advocate breastfeeding, but most opposed the risk approach. Like Taylor and Wallace (2012) who reject this approach as "shame-inducing," most of the respondents felt that focusing on medical, workplace, and cultural challenges women face would be a much more effective strategy, since it could actually change the environment in ways that are more compatible with breastfeeding.

These stories reveal that women view infant feeding decisions with an eye toward what is best for their families. They recognized others as doing the same, and resisted passing judgment on them. Impulses of choice and allowing others to do what they thought best were intermingled with support for changing the culture to be more supportive of breastfeeding. This appeared to stem from a recognition that "others have it harder" than they do.

Without some visible organizational movement that is focused on promoting cultural changes, they are unlikely to occur. Many woman spoke of policy changes that would be appropriate, but not of political activism as an avenue to change. There was discussion of what government or business ought to do, but not a sense of agency that they, as citizens, can demand change or work with others to achieve it. Some women shared a sense that mothering or parenting, in general, was not valued or supported enough in society; but they, for the most part, were not politicized as mothers or parents seeking to organize for change.

Two women involved with LLL did see some of the change (in terms of public breastfeeding norms) as being "completely grassroots." Asserting themselves and challenging the culture can help change that culture and give support to others by modeling a behavior that might be seen as inappropriate by some, in an effort to redefine those norms. Blum (1999) has suggested that norm-challenging behavior of this sort could be much more difficult or even dangerous for some groups of women in some contexts.

This leaves women making the best decisions they can, given the constraints they face, and allowing others to do the same. Chapters 4, 5, and 6 explore some of the current efforts that do exist to try to affect breastfeeding rates and infant feeding policy in the United States.

NOTES

1. See introduction for details on the sample and method. While quotes from the qualitative interviews are used through out the book to illustrate various perspectives and experiences, here I focus on the themes that emerged from these interviews in greater detail.

Chapter Four

Explaining Breastfeeding Rates in the States

Suzanne Barston (2012) writes of the pain and guilt she experienced when she was unable to continue to breastfeed her first child in California, where it seemed everyone was breastfeeding. It is not completely surprising that Barston felt the way she did given that 92.8 percent of babies born in 2011 were ever breastfed in California. On the other hand, in Louisiana 56.9 percent of babies born in 2011 were ever breastfed (see Table 4.1). Gaining a better understanding of the causes of this variation in breastfeeding rates across states can help improve policies designed to help parents carry out their infant feeding decisions.

This chapter addresses the question, "Which practices and policies most influence state breastfeeding rates?" The Centers for Disease Control (CDC) collects data on breastfeeding rates and medical variables that relate to breastfeeding. State laws aimed at protecting breastfeeding rights may also have an effect on breastfeeding rates. An analysis of factors most strongly related to breastfeeding can help health care personnel and state officials determine where to put resources in order to support breastfeeding.

This analysis is important in its own right. Regardless of one's position on the current approaches used in breastfeeding advocacy, most women don't meet their own breastfeeding goals. For example, 85 percent of women reported that they intended to breastfeed exclusively for three months, but only 32.4 percent of women with this goal were able to achieve it, according to an American Academy of Pediatrics study (Urban 2012). Surely an exploration of the policies and practices that best help women to breastfeed should be of concern to state policymakers and others concerned with supporting breastfeeding.

State Legislation Related to Breastfeeding

While many women breastfeed in public without incident, there are stories of women being asked to leave a store or coffee shop for breastfeeding (Kedrowski and Lipscomb 2008). Most states now have laws clarifying the right to breastfeed in public, though most of those laws do not include an enforcement provision (Marcus 2007). An enforcement provision can be a fine for violation of the law, a process for a woman to file a lawsuit in court, or a complaint with a state agency. This does not mean that breastfeeding in public is illegal in states without a law, but a woman could be asked to leave a privately owned business in the absence of an enforceable breastfeeding rights law. While some public breastfeeding laws are included in the state public accommodations law, others are not. Some laws simply state that women have the right to breastfeed in any public or private place they otherwise have a right to be. According to property law, owners and managers of public accommodations (privately owned businesses that are open to the public) can set their own rules of behavior and can refuse to serve anyone as long as they do not violate existing law (Marcus 2007; 2011).

Thus, a woman who is breastfeeding could potentially be asked to leave a public accommodation for any reason, which means she would no longer have a right to be there. Under property law, she can be transformed from a guest to a trespasser if she is asked to leave for any reason not otherwise prohibited by law (Marcus 2007; 2011; 2015). To prevent this, the optimal state laws create a right to breastfeed under the public accommodations law so that discrimination is clearly prohibited.

Some states have laws exempting breastfeeding from the public nudity laws, either instead of or in addition to a public breastfeeding law. Because so many states have passed breastfeeding rights legislation, the issue may appear to be uncontroversial. However, in some states the topic has been rather contentious. In Pennsylvania, for example, the proposed law was amended to permit breastfeeding rather than establish a right to breastfeed, due to explicit objections to creating a new right in the law. This led to some heated disagreement from supporters; the final language did not include this proposed change (Marcus 2015).

Two state laws have clauses that specify how breastfeeding must be performed. Missouri requires a woman to use as much discretion as possible; similarly North Dakota only protects "discreet" breastfeeding in public. This leaves "discreet" open to interpretation and could allow for harassment to occur. Marcus points out that this law actually makes breastfeeding illegal if it is not done discreetly. Arguably, this means the law actually provides less protection than no law at all (Marcus 2015).

Breastfeeding advocates oppose clauses requiring discreetness because they are subjective and open to interpretation. The absence of a state law protecting breastfeeding in public does not mean the action is against the law. Also, if a state only has a law excepting women from prosecution under indecent exposure laws, nursing mothers may not be protected from being asked to leave an establishment (Vance 2005). This type of law only provides protection from criminal prosecution for breastfeeding in public.

As of March 31, 2015, according to the National Council of State Legislatures, a total of forty-nine states had legislation that specifically protects breastfeeding in any public or private location:[1] twenty-nine states have laws exempting breastfeeding from the public indecency laws; twenty-five states have laws protecting breastfeeding in the workplace; and sixteen states allow breastfeeding women to be exempt from jury duty. Additionally, some states have passed other laws relating to breastfeeding. For example, Maryland exempts breastfeeding equipment and supplies for pumping breast milk from sales and use tax; Maine requires courts to consider whether children under the age of one year are being breastfed when deciding custody cases. Virginia has a law allowing breastfeeding on state property, but has recently passed more comprehensive legislation protecting breastfeeding in public that takes effect on July 1, 2015. (NCSL 2015).

Workplace legislation also varies greatly from state to state. The laws in California, Illinois, Minnesota, and Tennessee require employers to provide reasonable break-time and make reasonable efforts to provide a place to pump breast milk, unless the breaks would unduly disrupt operations. In Rhode Island, the law only states that employers may provide breaks for this purpose. Hawaii and Connecticut's laws do not require extra breaks for breastfeeding, but they state that women cannot be prohibited from using their existing breaks for this purpose. These laws prohibit employers from taking action or discriminating against such employees. California's law was the first to include fines for violations of its workplace accommodations law (Vance 2005). As with public breastfeeding laws, most states do not have an enforcement provision for workplace pumping laws. The federal workplace pumping law included in the Affordable Care Act also does not have an enforcement provision and does not apply to salaried employees. Additionally, businesses employing less than fifty employees may be exempt if they can show the requirement will create an undue hardship. The federal law applies across states; but if states have stricter laws, they apply in that state (Marcus 2011).

To measure state laws related to breastfeeding, I created an index that is simply the number of laws a state has from the major categories tracked by the National Conference of State Legislatures (NCSL). These laws include public indecency exemption, public breastfeeding, workplace pumping, jury duty exemption, and a state education campaign (see Table 4.1).

The most common state laws either create a right to breastfeed in public or exempt breastfeeding from the public nudity laws. Because the laws vary

Table 4.1 State Breastfeeding Rates for 2011 Births and State Legislation

State	Any Breastfeeding	Breastfeeding Six Months	# of State Laws Protecting Breastfeeding	Strength of Public Breastfeeding Law
California	92.8	63.1	4	2
Oregon	91.9	64.4	3	2
Washington	91.8	64.2	3	3
Montana	91.2	50.7	3	2
Vermont	90	66.5	3	3
Utah	89.6	63.1	1	1
Hawaii	89.5	61.5	2	3
Minnesota	89.2	59.2	4	2
Wyoming	87.6	56.6	3	2
Alaska	87.3	64.3	3	2
New Hampshire	86.4	57.6	2	3
Idaho	84.4	56.8	1	0
Wisconsin	83.5	54.9	2	3
Connecticut	83.3	51.4	2	3
Nebraska	82.4	46.1	2	2
North Dakota	82.4	55.4	3	1
Iowa	82.1	51.6	2	2
Maine	81.7	50.5	2	2
Arizona	81.6	47.8	2	2
New Jersey	81.6	56.2	1	3
Mass	81.4	53.7	2	3
Colorado	81	55.2	2	2
Nevada	80.9	45.3	2	2
New York	80.5	55.8	3	2
Virginia	80.5	53.7	3	2
Maryland	79.8	60.1	1	2
Rhode Island	79.7	47	3	3
Texas	78.4	42.9	2	2
South Dakota	77.7	45.6	1	2
Illinois	77.4	47	5	2
Kansas	77.4	40.3	2	2

State	Any Breastfeeding	Breastfeeding Six Months	# of State Laws Protecting Breastfeeding	Strength of Public Breastfeeding Law
North Carolina	77.2	48.3	2	2
Florida	77	48.7	2	2
New Mexico	76.9	45.9	2	2
Michigan	75.3	46.6	3	1
Tennessee	74.9	40.7	3	1
Indiana	74.1	38.6	2	2
South Carolina	73.4	37.4	2	2
Pennsylvania	72.9	45.7	2	2
Oklahoma	71.2	38.4	4	2
Georgia	70.3	40.1	2	2
Ohio	70.1	42.1	1	2
Missouri	67.9	42.1	2	1
Alabama	67.3	32.1	1	2
Arkansas	67.1	32.8	2	2
Delaware	65.7	34.4	1	2
Mississippi	61.5	28.9	3	2
Kentucky	61.3	31.5	3	2
West Virginia	59.3	29.3	1	1
Louisiana	56.9	30.3	2	3

Note: Sorted by Any breastfeeding from highest to lowest state.

Sources: Centers for Disease Control 2011 Births from 2014 Breastfeeding Report Card; National Conference of State Legislatures 2015; Jake Marcus. *Breastfeeding Law: Know Your Legal Rights,* "State Laws" at breastfeedinglaw.com; Statistical Abstract of the United States 2013.

so much, I created a scale to measure the strength of public breastfeeding protection in each state. It ranges from 1 to 3, with a "1" being the weakest type of law that either only exempts the practice from being considered a crime, or grants a limited or qualified right to breastfeed in public. Those states rated "2" are those with a law that grants the right to breastfeed in public without limitations or qualifications, but with no specified penalty for violators. States rated "3" have all the same specifications as those rated a "2," plus an enforcement provision that specifies a penalty for violating the law or a process for bringing civil action against the violator of the law (Marcus 2015; see Table 4.1).

While the legal environment for breastfeeding in a state may have an effect on breastfeeding rates, I expect medical and civil society variables to have the strongest relationship with breastfeeding rates.

Medical Practices and Resources

How are breastfeeding rates affected by medical practices, personnel, and hospital policies within a state? Because the majority of women currently give birth in a hospital in the United States, breastfeeding most often begins there. Historians argue that hospital practices played a role in the decline of breastfeeding in the 1930s and 1940s when more women began birthing in hospitals instead of at home (Apple 1987; Wright 2001). Variation across states in terms of hospital practices that help support breastfeeding is high (CDC 2014) and may continue to play a major role in affecting breastfeeding rates and duration.

The mPINC survey on maternity practices in infant nutrition and care offers a great source of data for state-level analysis. The CDC (2014) provides an average mPINC score for each state. This statistic was reported in the 2014 Breastfeeding Report Card, which reports data for 2011 births. The survey is scored on a scale of 0 to 100, with 100 being the highest score (most supportive of breastfeeding). Some items included in the score are as follows: support to breastfeeding women, skin-to-skin contact, whether breastfed infants are given formula in the first two days, and whether breastfeeding families are given pacifiers and formula samples in the hospital. Medical experts specializing in breastfeeding argue that supportive practices in the hospital lead to both higher initiation rates and duration rates, so states with higher average scores are expected to have higher breastfeeding rates (see Table 4.2).

A related medical variable reported by the CDC is the percentage of babies born in hospitals with the designation, "Baby-Friendly." According to UNICEF's website, the Baby-Friendly Hospital Initiative (BFHI) was launched by the World Health Organization (WHO) and UNICEF in 1991. In order to receive the designation, hospitals and birth centers must not accept free or reduced price formula and must implement ten steps that support breastfeeding, including providing training to staff and not giving formula or other liquids to breastfeeding babies unless medically indicated (UNICEF 2014). The CDC records the percentage of births in hospitals with the designation by state, which is predicted to have a direct effect on state breastfeeding rates (see Table 4.2).

Finally, the CDC (2014) also reports the number of International Board Certified Lactation Consultants (IBCLCs) per 1000 live births in its annual report card. Women living in states with a higher number of IBCLCs should have access to greater breastfeeding support than those in states with fewer

Table 4.2: State Breastfeeding Rates and Breastfeeding Support Indicators for 2011 Births

State	Any Breastfeeding	Breastfeeding for Six Months	Average mPINC Score	Percentage of Births at Baby Friendly Hospitals
California	92.8	63.1	83	26.97
Oregon	91.9	64.4	85	9.21
Washington	91.8	64.2	82	11.18
Montana	91.2	50.7	80	0.25
Vermont	90	66.5	88	3.21
Utah	89.6	63.1	72	6.43
Hawaii	89.5	61.5	80	8.94
Minnesota	89.2	59.2	77	8.23
Wyoming	87.6	56.6	71	2.85
Alaska	87.3	64.3	82	21.79
New Hampshire	86.4	57.6	91	35.98
Idaho	84.4	56.8	76	7.26
Wisconsin	83.5	54.9	79	12.43
Connecticut	83.3	51.4	82	28.56
Nebraska	82.4	46.1	68	7.49
North Dakota	82.4	55.4	75	2.01
Iowa	82.1	51.6	69	0.14
Maine	81.7	50.5	82	27.56
Arizona	81.6	47.8	75	1.65
New Jersey	81.6	56.2	78	5.96
Mass	81.4	53.7	84	7.12
Colorado	81	55.2	79	8.6
Nevada	80.9	45.3	71	5.2
New York	80.5	55.8	80	5.72
Virginia	80.5	53.7	76	0.52
Maryland	79.8	60.1	76	6.77
Rhode Island	79.7	47	86	10.53
Texas	78.4	42.9	73	3.35
South Dakota	77.7	45.6	70	3.91
Illinois	77.4	47	77	2.55

State	Any Breastfeeding	Breastfeeding for Six Months	Average mPINC Score	Percentage of Births at Baby Friendly Hospitals
Kansas	77.4	40.3	70	0
North Carolina	77.2	48.3	75	9.75
Florida	77	48.7	78	2.57
New Mexico	76.9	45.9	77	3.77
Michigan	75.3	46.6	73	0.5
Tennessee	74.9	40.7	67	0.13
Indiana	74.1	38.6	76	12.01
South Carolina	73.4	37.4	78	9.25
Pennsylvania	72.9	45.7	74	0.08
Oklahoma	71.2	38.4	71	0.4
Georgia	70.3	40.1	69	0
Ohio	70.1	42.1	76	10.31
Missouri	67.9	42.1	71	0.82
Alabama	67.3	32.1	67	2.5
Arkansas	67.1	32.8	62	0
Delaware	65.7	34.4	86	8.41
Mississippi	61.5	28.9	59	0
Kentucky	61.3	31.5	70	5.85
West Virginia	59.3	29.3	69	0
Louisiana	56.9	30.3	71	0

Note: Sorted by Any Breastfeeding variable from highest to lowest state.

Sources: Centers for Disease Control data for 2011 Births from 2014 Breastfeeding Report Card

IBCLCs. Hospitals in the states with more IBCLCs should have more of them on staff; generally, it should be easier to get an appointment with an IBCLC in these states (see Table 4.2).

Civil Society

La Leche League International (LLL) is a non-profit organization that has provided mother-to-mother support to breastfeeding women since it was founded in 1956. It is open to anyone seeking breastfeeding information and advice. Those who attend monthly meetings are under no obligation to join the organization, though they can join for a small fee ($25.00 dues annually for a basic membership). Women are routinely referred to the organization for support with breastfeeding. This can fill a real need for women who may not need a lactation consultant, but are looking for some basic support. It also provides a community for breastfeeding women who, in some areas, may feel they are doing something that not everyone is doing, especially in public (LLL 2010). The measure for this variable is the number of LLL leaders per 1000 births (see Table 4.2).

Controls: Demographic Variables

The demographic make-up of a state has an impact on its breastfeeding rates. CDC data show that states with higher rates of education have higher levels of breastfeeding. Also, states with a higher percentage of African Americans have lower breastfeeding rates compared to states with a lower percentage of African Americans. While much of the increase in U.S. breastfeeding rates during the 1990s has been due to an increase in breastfeeding rates among African Americans, their overall rates are still lower than those for whites. Since demographic factors could be rival explanations for variation in state breastfeeding rates, they are included as control variables in the analysis (CDC 2014; Wright 2001).

Data Analysis

I examined breastfeeding rates at the state level to determine which medical, legal, and civil society variables are most correlated with breastfeeding rates. For breastfeeding advocates, this analysis is helpful in the quest to increase breastfeeding rates. For feminists and others with concerns that some groups face more constraints to breastfeeding than others, this analysis can provide some insights as to where to focus efforts to promote policies and medical practices that support women who already want to breastfeed, to enable them to be successful in meeting their goals. The question of whether legal, medical, or civil society variables affect breastfeeding rates is an important one. Exploring this question can help state officials decide where to focus their efforts. Using correlational and regression analysis, I test the following hypotheses using the CDC 2014 Breastfeeding Report Card data for 2011 births as well as data on state laws from NCSL and Attorney Jake Marcus's "State Laws" page on her website, http://www.breastfeedinglaw.com.

Legislative Hypotheses

- States with more breastfeeding laws will have higher breastfeeding rates than states with fewer breastfeeding laws.

- States with stronger laws protecting public breastfeeding will have higher breastfeeding rates than states with weaker laws protecting public breast-feeding.

Medical Resources and Practices Hypotheses

- States with higher mPINC scores will have higher rates of breastfeeding than states with lower mPINC scores.
- States with greater numbers of IBCLCs per 1000 live births will have higher breastfeeding rates than states with fewer IBCLCs per 1000 births.
- States with a higher percentage of babies born in hospitals with the WHO/ UNICEF designation, Baby-Friendly, will have higher breastfeeding rates that those without the designation.

Civil Society Hypothesis

- States with higher numbers of La Leche League Leaders per 1000 live births will have higher breastfeeding rates.

Demographic Hypothesis

- States with a higher percentage of the population holding a four-year college degree will have higher rates of breastfeeding.
- States with higher percentages of African Americans will have lower breastfeeding rates.

Results

I analyzed the relationship between the legislative, medical, civil society, and demographic variables described above and the dependent variable, percentage of 2011 births breastfeeding at six months.[2] I used Pearson's r correlation coefficients to measure the strength of the relationship between the variables. The results show that medical variables supporting breastfeeding are correlated with state breastfeeding rates at six months, while neither of the legislative variables correlate with breastfeeding rates (see Table 4.3). The strongest correlation is the measure of hospital practices (mPINC scores) with a highly significant Pearson's r of .6232 (Sig. = .0000). Coming in second, is the IBCLC rate at .5411, which is also highly significant (Sig. =.0000).

The last medical variable, percentage of births in hospitals with the Baby-Friendly designation, is also significant with a Pearson's r of .4057 (Sig. = .0035). The Baby-Friendly Hospital variable is not as highly correlated with breastfeeding rates as the civil society variable, La Leche League Leaders per

Table 4.3: State Level Variables: Correlations with Breastfeeding at Six Months

State breastfeeding variables	Pearson's R	Statistical Significance
Average state mPINC Score	.6232	.0000
IBCLCs per 1000 births	.5411	.0000
Percentage of the population with a college degree	.5264	.0001
Percentage of population that is African American 2010	-.5202	.0001
La Leche League Leaders per 1000 births	.4254	.0021
Percent of births in hospitals with Baby-Friendly designation	.4057	.0035
Number of state breastfeeding laws	.1981	.1678
Strength of state public breastfeeding laws	.1568	.2768

Sources: Centers for Disease Control 2011 Births from 2014 Breastfeeding Report Card; National Conference of State Legislatures 2015; Jake Marcus. *Breastfeeding Law: Know Your Legal Rights,* "State Laws" at breastfeedinglaw.com; Statistical Abstract of the United States 2013

1000 live births, with a correlation of .4254 (Sig. = 0021). The two control variables are correlated with breastfeeding rates, with a Pearson's r of .5264 (Sig. = .0001) for the percentage of the population with a college degree, and -.5202 (Sig. = .0001) for the percentage of the population who is African American. All of the correlations are in the direction predicted by the hypotheses.

Since the correlational analysis does not control for the other variables related to breastfeeding, I use Ordinary Least Squares regression to determine if the significantly correlated variables are causally related to breastfeeding rates. The regression coefficients (b) reported in each model show the amount of change in breastfeeding rates caused by each independent variable, while controlling for the effects of each of the others.

Since mPINC scores were the most highly correlated with breastfeeding rates, Model 1 reports just the bivariate regression for this variable (see Table 4.4). This single variable explains 38 percent of the variation in six-month breastfeeding rates (adjusted R^2=.38). The model is statistically significant with an F statistic of 30.47.

Models 2–4 are also presented in Table 4.4. IBCLC rates, LLL leader rates and mPINC scores are placed in separate models due to problems with multicollinearity among these variables.[3] The model statistics show that all three multivariate models are statistically significant. The adjusted R^2s show that the independent variables in the models explain about half of the variation in breastfeeding rates across states, with Model 2, (which includes mPINC scores) explaining the most (R^2=.5213).

Model 2 shows that mPINC scores remain statistically significant when controlling for the other variables (see Table 4.4). The coefficient is .5372, which indicates that for each one point increase in mPINC scores, the breastfeeding rate increases by just over one-half of a percentage point. In Model 3, the regression coefficient for the IBCLC rate indicates that for each additional IBCLC per 1000 births, the breastfeeding rate increases by over one percentage point (b=1.3012). In Model 4, only the demographic variables are statistically significant. The variable for La Leche League Leaders per 1000

Table 4.4: Ordinary Least Squares Regression of State Factors on Breast-feeding at Six Months

State Breastfeeding Variables	Model 1	Model 2	Model 3	Model 4
Average state PINC Score	.9798*** (.1775)	.5372* (.2264)		
% of state births in hospitals with Baby Friendly designation		.0602 (.1616)	.1771 (.1423)	.2530 (.1390)
% of population that is African American		-.3497** (.1139)	-.3540** (.1156)	-.3814** (.1180)
% of population with College Degree		.4411** (.1782)	.5620** (.1706)	.5919** (.1772)
Number of IBCLCs per 1000 live births			1.3012* (.6270)	
La Leche League Leaders per 1000 live births				2.478 (2.049)
Intercept	-25.7438	15.4485	6.8166	25.3338
Adj. R^2	.3883	.5213	.5058	.4784
F	30.47***	14.34***	13.67***	12.23***
N	df (1. 48) 50	df(5, 45) 50	df(4, 45) 50	df(5, 45) 50

Source: Centers for Disease Control and Prevention (CDC) Breastfeeding Report Card 2014

Note: Standard errors in parentheses. *p< .05, **p<.01, ***p<.001

births does not reach statistical significance when controlling for the other variables.

In all three multivariate models, the demographic variables show statistically significant effects. The regression coefficients show that for each one percent increase in college graduates in the state population, breastfeeding rates increase by roughly a half of a percentage point. The effects for race are also fairly consistent across models. For each one percent increase in the state population that is African American, breastfeeding rates decrease by a little more than a third of one percent (see Table 4.4). The Baby Friendly Hospital variable does not reach statistical significance in any of the multivariate models.

Discussion and Conclusions

Despite the passage of many laws protecting breastfeeding in a relatively short amount of time, the results show no direct effect on breastfeeding rates (at least for the data analyzed here). The weak showing of the public breastfeeding laws variable may also be due to the fact that many women report not having ever been asked not to breastfeed in public, though this does not mean the laws are not valuable in terms of protecting individuals from harassment (Stearns 1999).[4] It may be that the laws affect public breastfeeding practices at the individual level; but this would be difficult to study systematically.

In my field interviews, as discussed in chapter 3, I found many women were not even aware there was a law in their state giving them the right to breastfeed in public. Some stated that they just assumed they could breastfeed where they wished, while others reported that they felt uncomfortable and tried to avoid it. None of the women expressed any doubts about whether it was legal, and none of the women felt it was inappropriate or should be illegal. If many women who are breastfeeding are not aware of state laws regarding breastfeeding in public, then it is unlikely these laws are affecting state breastfeeding rates.

The state breastfeeding laws also may not have an effect on breastfeeding rates because they are being ignored. Many of the stories of women who have been asked to leave public places have occurred in states that do have public breastfeeding laws.[5] Most of these laws still do not have an enforcement provision, which means there is no consequence for violating them. This is also true of workplace pumping laws as well, and may cause them to be equally ineffective in raising breastfeeding rates (Marcus 2007; 2010).

Another reason the laws may not have much of an effect is culture. Laws are often not followed when they are not accepted by the public as legitimate. This may also lead to laws not being enforced (Meier 1994). One example is the routine violation of speed limits when no traffic cameras or police are present. Urban planners have pointed out that drivers simply do what seems safe given the road width and conditions, rather than following posted speed limits (Duany, Plater-Zyberk and Speck 2000). If breastfeeding in public remains rare, some people may continue to equate it with other bodily functions not done in public, i.e. urinating and defecating, rather than the commonly public function of eating. Perhaps the regional culture matters more than any laws that may be on the books.

This may create a bit of a catch twenty-two situation, where in order for more women to feel comfortable breastfeeding in public, more women need to breastfeed in public, with the law not really having much effect one way or the other. Some have suggested that state breastfeeding education campaigns target the public, instead of just breastfeeding women (Kedrowski and Lipscomb 2008). At the end of the day, dominant cultural norms probably shape behavior in the public space more than laws, though they may help to change perspectives over time.

While the Baby-Friendly designation has some similar criteria to the mPINC score, the weak showing of the former may be related to the fact that a hospital either gets the designation for meeting all the criteria, or fails to get the designation. With the mPINC score, a hospital gets credit for all the practices it engages in that support breastfeeding, even if it fails to get the Baby-Friendly designation. One reason a hospital may not get the designation is if it accepts free or reduced price formula or if it passes out free formula to patients leaving the hospital. Because many hospitals may feel they need to accept these deals in order to keep costs down, this may lead to hospitals not getting the designation even if they comply with many of the other requirements.

Given the results presented here, states should focus primarily on raising mPINC scores and increasing the number of IBCLCs. State officials can do this by providing incentives and resources to hospitals in the area of lactation. Also, IBCLC training can be prioritized by states with lower rates. State breastfeeding coalitions, for example, offer financial assistance and mentorship programs to those seeking to sit for the IBCLC exam; these programs could be expanded with additional funding. Since many IBCLCs work in hospitals, it is not surprising that their presence is associated with higher mPINC scores. Focusing on mPINC scores should not pose any risk to infants requiring formula, because the criteria exempt medically necessary supplementation.

Also, a focus on raising state mPINC scores should not cause women to be coerced into breastfeeding since the criteria focus on the training of staff and support of women who are breastfeeding, rather than on pushing the uninterested to breastfeed. Requirements not to provide pacifiers, for example, only apply to those infants who are breastfed rather than to all infants. Since many women do not meet their own breastfeeding goals, a focus on hospital and birth center practices should be viewed as helping women meet the goals they have set for themselves, rather than pressuring women to breastfeed.

Future Research

While this analysis shows the importance of IBCLC rates and hospital and birth center practices (measured by mPINC scores) for supporting breast-feeding in the states, future study at the state level could determine if other policies less directly related to breastfeeding have an impact on breastfeeding rates.

Throughout this book I argue that policies that support care work more generally could go a long way to make breastfeeding possible for those who may wish to do it, but face work and family challenges. State paid family leave is another policy that could lead to higher breastfeeding rates as it would allow breastfeeding women to spend more time with their babies in the first few months after birth. Women going back to work after three months tend to have fewer issues with milk supply than those who return earlier. Family leave for fathers can also support breastfeeding by allowing men to take up other care responsibilities, making breastfeeding more manageable for their co-parent.

Paid state family leave also provides an option for women who would like to breastfeed but find the prospect of pumping several times a day for many months, daunting or incompatible with their occupations. While evidence from states with paid family leave show some positive effects on breastfeeding, only three states currently have this policy. Therefore, it could not be included in the analysis (NCSL 2013). This is a variable that could be explored in the future if the trend continues toward states adopting this policy. Eight other states do currently have their own leave policies. Most of these go beyond the federal Family and Medical Leave Act in terms of categories of workers covered, or length of time covered, but do not offer paid leave. Future research could explore the effects of these policies as well to see if they contribute to higher state breastfeeding rates (NCSL 2013).

NOTES

1. Utah is included in the count, though it is not a statewide law and only prohibits county ordinances banning public breastfeeding, Utah Code Ann. § 17-15-25 (1995).

2. Analysis using other dependent variables, such as the exclusive 6-months breastfeeding rate, initiation (or every breastfed) rate, and twelve-month rate, gave very similar results. I presented the six-months number because it shows sustained breastfeeding without excluding those infants who may be mostly breastfed but, for whatever reason, have had some formula or may have started solids before six months.

3. Variance Inflation Factors were all under 4, but VIFs for these variables when included together were twice as high as the other variables. Standard errors became inflated as well, which is a sign of multicollinearity.

4. Also see the results of personal interviews in chapter three.
5. See chapter six for a detailed discussion of these stories.

Chapter Five

Medical and Public Health Approaches to Breastfeeding Advocacy

When I was pregnant with my daughter in 2004, I was watching television one night with my husband and saw a public service announcement related to breastfeeding. Since I was planning to breastfeed, I expected to be in full agreement with it, but my husband and I were rather surprised by what we saw. A woman who looked about eight or nine months pregnant was riding a mechanical bull in a bar with a crowd cheering her on. Then a voice said, "You wouldn't take risks before your baby was born, why start after?" The voice continued to list the reduction in illness associated with breastfeeding, followed by the statement "Babies were born to be breastfed." Next, "Breastfeed exclusively for six months" appeared across the screen. While I was unaware of it at the time, the ad was part of the National Breastfeeding Awareness Campaign that was sponsored by the Ad Council and the United States Department of Health and Human Services (HHS), Office of Women's Health, which was funded in order to carry out the HHS 2000 Call for Action on Breastfeeding (Boswell-Penc 2006).

Breastfeeding is identified as a major public health issue by both the American Academy of Pediatrics (AAP) and HHS. The former has issued several statements recommending breastfeeding over the past few decades, while the latter has set goals in 2000 and again in 2010 for increasing the frequency and duration of breastfeeding. This chapter explores public health and general medical approaches to promoting breastfeeding and how they have changed over time in the United States. An analysis of government and AAP documents going back to the 1940s demonstrates that while those writing about breastfeeding in the medical community argued that breastfeeding was beneficial as early as the 1940s, they also demonstrated a lack of understanding of the practices that make lactation successful and helped to create a

social environment that they are now trying to undo; namely one which largely treats formula feeding as the default, and breastfeeding as a beneficial bonus (Apple 1987; Dunham and Crane 1943) .

Two major approaches to advocacy have been identified in the analysis of AAP and government documents promoting breastfeeding. The first is the *breast is best* approach or *benefits* approach, emphasizing advantages of breastfeeding, while the latter is the risk approach advocated by Wiessinger (2001), Wight (1999), and others. The idea of the risk approach is that the language be turned around to stress the risks of using formula, rather than the benefits of breastfeeding. This approach starts with the assumption of breast-feeding as the default, and then compares breastfed infants with those fed formula, rather than making the comparison the other way around and talking about the health benefits of breastfeeding.

Government Public Health Initiatives

In a 2000 Call to Action document, the Surgeon General calls breastfeeding "the most important contributor to infant health." Low rates of breastfeeding are cited as a public health challenge that the nation must address through "national, culturally appropriate strategies" (HHS 2000). The Office of the Surgeon General held its first workshop on breastfeeding and lactation in 1984. Goals were set to improve professional and public education, provide more support in the health care system for breastfeeding, develop community support, promote breastfeeding among working women, and to expand research on lactation.

In 2000, the Healthy People Initiative was put into place to achieve breastfeeding goals by 2010. Again, breastfeeding goals have been set in 2010 to be reached by 2020 as part of the broader public health initiatives of the Healthy People 2020 program now underway. Annual Breastfeeding Report Cards have been issued by the CDC since 2007, tracking breastfeeding rates at various stages of infancy for each state, as well as nationally. Percentages are reported for infants born in each year who are ever breastfed, breastfed at three months, six months, and twelve months. These figures include infants who may also receive formula in addition to being nursed at the breast. Measures for exclusive breastfeeding are reported for three months and six months. The goal for 2020 for any breastfeeding is 81.9 percent; the national figure reported for 2011 births is 79.2 percent (CDC 2014). This number drops to 49 percent breastfeeding at six months (16.4 percent for exclusively breastfeeding at six months).

An Analysis of American Academy of Pediatrics Recommendations on Breastfeeding

The American Academy of Pediatrics (AAP) was founded in 1930 in Elk Grove, Illinois, where it is headquartered today. The journal of the AAP, *Pediatrics,* was first published in 1948. According to the 1997 article, "Breastfeeding and the Use of Human Milk" published by the Work Group on Breastfeeding, the organization has promoted breastfeeding since its founding and states that the manual, *Standards and Recommendations for the Hospital Care of Newborn Infants* of 1948 recommended that every mother be encouraged to breastfeed her full-term newborn (AAP 1997).

I reviewed an online copy of an earlier manual with the same title, published as a government document by the Department of Labor, Children's Bureau, which had been reviewed by the AAP and authored by Dr. Ethel C. Dunham and Dr. Marian M. Crane. The manual states, "It is recommended that every effort be made to have every mother of a full-term infant nurse him" (Dunham and Crane 1943, 12). It then goes on in a section entitled, "Breastfeeding Technique" (where one might expect to read about latching the infant onto the breast and various positions or holds), stating that the mother must wash her hands and breasts with soap and water before nursing. It is also recommended that sterilized water be given to infants before the mother's milk comes in and periodically between feedings (Dunham and Crane 1943). It is noteworthy that the recommendation begins on page twelve of the manual and is followed directly by a section on preparing milk mixtures and handling bottles. Additionally, the manual contains a longer section on pages five and six, before the breastfeeding recommendation labeled "Milk Room," that describes the configuration and sterile procedures for the work area for "making up feedings" with no reference to breastfeeding whatsoever (Dunham and Crane 1943, 5).

In this manual, I encountered the same procedures Rima Apple writes about in describing the scientific motherhood approach in her book, *Mothers and Medicine.* While encouraging each mother to breastfeed, there seems to be an underlying assumption that she won't, combined with recommended hospital procedures that will undermine it if she tries, such as bottles of water in between feedings and repeated breast washings (Apple 1987, 120).

It is not surprising to find a concern with cleanliness and sterilization in a hospital setting in 1943, since the first antibiotics were not widely available until the mid- to late-1940s (AAP 2014). Also, since high infant mortality around the turn of the century was attributed partly to unclean feeding conditions, there appeared to be an assumption that this same obsession with cleanliness was needed for breastfeeding. On the one hand, this is understandable since the scientific understanding of breast milk and its infection-fighting properties was not yet fully understood. However, the public health

campaigns in major cities, to encourage mothers to breastfeed at higher rates around the turn of the twentieth century (before infants were primarily born in hospitals) should have been known to physicians; yet this earlier campaign was not accompanied by the same obsession with cleanliness of the breast (Wolf 2003). This document shows how a practice that was routinely done by women for centuries, with the help of other women, was medicalized and made problematic when hospital births became routine and much of that previous knowledge was marginalized.

Since 1997, the Work Group on Breastfeeding (now called the Section on Breastfeeding) has published statements in the AAP's journal, *Pediatrics*. The statement was updated in 2005 and in 2012. The 1997 statement represented a change from earlier Work Group recommendations in that it was an article-length policy statement formally published in the journal of *Pediatrics*. The benefits of breastfeeding for the infant and mother are detailed in the statement with citations to the medical studies that demonstrate these effects.

The 1997 statement discusses the *benefits* of breastfeeding and its superior quality over formula, right after stating that the breasted infant is the normative standard. This is rather contradictory. The excerpt reads, "The breastfed infant is the reference or normative model against which all alternative feeding methods must be measured with regard to growth, health, development, and all other short- and long-term outcomes" (1035). This is immediately followed by the statement, "Epidemiologic research shows that human milk and breastfeeding of infants provide advantages with regard to general health, growth, and development, while significantly decreasing risk for a large number of acute and chronic diseases" (AAP 1997, 1035). If a breastfed infant is the reference or normative model, after reading the above statement, one has to ask, "To what advantages do they refer?" This must refer to advantages over an infant that is fed formula. The AAP uses the formula-fed infant as the base-line starting point from which to judge differences, after stating that this is not the correct standard.

The 2005 statement also refers to exclusive breastfeeding as the normative model from which all other feeding methods must be judged, but then goes on to use infants who are not breastfed as the default standard. For example:

> Research in developed and developing countries of the world, including middle-class populations in developed countries, provides strong evidence that human milk feeding *decreases* the incidence and/or severity of a wide range of infectious diseases, including bacterial meningitis, bacteremia, diarrhea, respiratory tract infection, necrotizing enterocolitis, otitis media, urinary tract infection, and late-onset sepsis in preterm infants. In addition, postneonatal infant mortality rates in the United States are *reduced* by 21 percent in breastfed infants. (AAP 2005, 496; italics added)

If breastfeeding is decreasing incidence of disease, then the baseline being used here is obviously an infant not fed breast milk. Why the insistence that breastfeeding is the normative standard, if all the comparisons are made as if formula is the standard? What makes this language so hard to avoid?

The language of the 2012 AAP policy makes greater use of the term *risk*; for example the abstract states, "Pediatricians play a critical role in their practices and communities as advocates of breastfeeding and thus should be knowledgeable about the health risks of not breastfeeding, the economic benefits to society of breastfeeding, and the techniques for managing and supporting the breastfeeding dyad" (AAP e827).

However, despite this statement in the abstract of the document, the findings reported in the document itself tend to focus on the *reduced* risk of disease when infants are breastfed, rather than starting from breastfed infants and stating that formula *increases* risk as with the statement in the abstract. For example the document states, "Any breastfeeding is associated with a 64 percent *reduction* in the incidence of nonspecific gastrointestinal tract infections, and this effect lasts for 2 months after cessation of breastfeeding" (AAP 2012, e829; italics added). The findings relating to Type I and II Diabetes, Celiac's Disease, obesity, allergies, leukemia and lymphoma, inflammatory bowel disease, ear infections, respiratory tract infections, and Sudden Infant Death Syndrome also are all written in terms of a reduction in risk for breastfed infants, rather than increased risk of these diseases for formula-fed infants (AAP 2012, e828-e830). While the findings are important to report and the differences between the groups often large, the direction of the language is puzzling given the opening statements in the 1997, 2005, and 2012 abstracts asserting breastfeeding as the normative standard against which all other feeding methods should be compared and the emphasis on the risks of not breastfeeding.

The Risk Approach in HHS Documents

An analysis of documents from the Office of the Surgeon General from the first 1985 report through 2012 shows a shift to some use of *risk* language, which states that women put their infants at greater risk for various illnesses when they use formula. In the document, *Doctors in Action: A Call to Action from the Surgeon General to Support Breastfeeding*, under the section entitled "Support Mothers Decisions," the document reads, "Many mothers do not know the health risks to their babies and themselves when they do not breastfeed" (HHS 2011a). On the other hand, another HHS document from the same year, the Executive Summary, from the series *The Surgeon General's Call to Action to Support Breastfeeding*, states, "The decision to breastfeed is a personal one and a mother should not be made to feel guilty if she cannot or chooses not to breastfeed" (HHS 2011b).

Analyzing the Risk Approach to Advocacy

One might argue that I am "splitting-hairs" or that none of this really matters, because the bottom line is that breast milk leads to fewer gastrointestinal infections and reduced risk of other diseases. Why such analysis of *risk* versus *benefit* language and whether one chooses to write about reducing risks with breastfeeding versus increasing risks with formula? The choice of language is telling because it continues the pattern (though to a much lesser degree) that is seen in the 1943 document (Dunham and Crane 1943) where breastfeeding is briefly recommended before the manual continues as if for-mula feeding was the norm, because it *was the norm* in terms of practice, and a sentence recommending breastfeeding could not and did not change that.

The continued return to the benefits language or even talk of reduced risks due to breastfeeding assumes formula-feeding as the baseline, even though all of the AAP statements have asserted since 1997 that the breastfed infant is the normative standard. If breastfeeding really were the normative standard then the statements would report the increased risks associated with formula use rather than the decreased risks associated with breastfeeding, without even having to think about it. The writer reverts to benefits language when he or she goes into detail, as this language feels the most natural to those researching and writing about the topic because it reflects their actual experience in the United States, where the *actual norm in practice* is to see an infant with a bottle, not an infant at the breast.

Some might argue that this is just a cultural norm and not the biological norm; yet human beings draw conclusions from lived experience and, empir-ically, most infants are not breastfed exclusively for most of their first year (CDC 2014). Insisting on a norm one would like to see, even if it seems most biologically appropriate does not create a norm; people breastfeeding for substantial lengths of time creates a norm since human beings are cultural and social creatures, not just biological ones. We may be mammals, but we are mammals who invented and have been using bottles and formula with great frequency for quite some time.

The problem is that simply saying something over and over does not make it so. Breastfeeding rates in the United States show that while the vast majority of infants (79.2 percent for 2011 births) are breastfed at least once in the hospital, the majority of infants are not breastfed at all at six months, with 49.4 percent breast-fed to some degree at this age. Only 40.7 percent are exclusively breastfed at 3 months, and 18.8 percent are fed only breast milk at six months. By one-year, only 26 percent are doing any breastfeeding (CDC 2014). While breastfeeding initiation rates have been increasing over time, duration rates demonstrate that most infants are not exclusively fed breast milk for the first six months, as the AAP recommends. It took many decades and many participants to move from a majority of infants being mostly breastfed in 1900, to 78 percent of infants being fed only formula in 1972; simply asserting that breastfeeding is the normative standard will not change that.

Using the formula-fed infant as the baseline *just feels appropriate* (apparently, even to physicians in the AAP Section on Breastfeeding or perhaps to the researchers in the original studies cited) because of these statistics and what we all see when we go out to malls, live our lives, or just spend time with families in the broader culture, outside of La Leche League and Attachment Parenting International. The statistics tell us where we actually are; this is important because wherever it is we wish to go, we have to start from where we are. It is understandable, from a medical point of view, to argue that breastfeeding should be the normative standard since it was the original or biologic norm in the same way that not being exposed to tobacco smoke or air pollution from factories was the biologic norm for humans. With no adequate substitute, babies were fed with breast milk (though not always by their own mothers). Humans thrived on it for a very long time before formula came along, but come along it did.

It is important to note that dramatic improvements in health were increasing at the same time that formula use became routine. Since 1900, average life expectancy has increased from forty-seven years to seventy-eight years due to improvements in public health (CDC 1999). At the low point of breastfeeding rates (1972), life expectancy was already at 71.2 (CDC 2014). Kedrowski and Lipscomb (2008) point out that this may have masked some of the effects of the dramatic movement toward formula-use during this time. They argue that without these improvements, we might have been able to see a decline in health indicators during this time due to a decrease in breastfeeding; but due to the availability of antibiotics, vaccines, and other medical advances, dramatic improvements were seen instead.

Almost every woman I interviewed reacted negatively to the risks of formula language when I presented it to her for comment.[1] Why? They felt it would make women feel guilty, and that this would make them angry to the point where they might reject the advice altogether. I showed my college students the NBAC ads; not a single one thought they were part of an appropriate approach to promoting breastfeeding. On the other hand, when I showed them the CDC ads featuring Terrie Hall's story, every single student felt they were very powerful and appropriate for an anti-smoking campaign (CDC 2014).

Wiessinger (2001) and others have argued that no one can make anyone feel guilty, that it comes from within when individuals feel or know they have done something wrong. However, given the history of hospital practices that undermined breastfeeding even while recommending it, there is good reason for women to feel angry if they are made to feel guilty or that they shoulder all the blame for the decisions they make in imperfect conditions.

They do not want to be shamed for something that took an entire society to bring about. Women don't make choices in a vacuum; they make them within the context of a given culture and set of norms and expectations for behavior involving where infants sleep and for how long they are expected to sleep, as well as what they are fed and how often and what they should eat. Add to that the challenges of combining work and breastfeeding in a country where only 13 percent of workers receive any paid family leave at all. It is not difficult to see why people do not like the risk approach.

On the other hand, while I found breastfeeding mothers rejected the language of the risks of formula, they very much accepted the medical evidence for breastfeeding (See chapter 3). They did not question the benefits and cited them overwhelmingly as a major reason for breastfeeding. In other words, they did not reject the medical evidence, but rejected the idea that the breastfed infant actually is the correct normative standard from which to compare other infants, and the focus on individual mothers' behavior.

So, while Wiessinger argues that we need to "watch our language" in order to make breastfeeding the norm by speaking and writing as though it is the norm, I argue that it will not ring true unless it becomes the *actual* norm in terms of practice, for longer than a few weeks or months. *Risky* formula will also be a hard-sell to people who live in a country with a safe water supply, grocery shelves filled with a host of brands and types of formula to choose from (with no Surgeon General Warning like that which adorns the cigarette packages), and a federal government that remains the largest purchaser of infant formula fed to infants through the WIC program (Oliveiria, Frazao, and Smallwood 2011).

If cultural, employment, and medical barriers are keeping women who want to nurse from being able to do so, then certainly goals should be set to remove those barriers, but is *risk* the appropriate language to be used? In defending the risk approach, Wiessinger (2001) points out that the formula companies have started using the *Breast Is Best* language for a good reason. She argues that they know most of us don't expect to be perfect, optimal, or best because, after all, no one is perfect. Wiessinger argues that we need to turn things around and speak as if breastfeeding is the norm. Rather than talking about breastfeeding reducing risks of obesity, ear infection, and so on, we would instead state the increased risk of these conditions for babies who are fed formula.

In other words, she argues that we should discuss formula feeding in terms of risks in much the same way we talk about how smoking increases the risks of lung cancer. She says the goal is not to make women feel guilty, but rather to save them from a life of regret if they were to find out later that they could have prevented problems in their child. However, if we examine one of the early passages from the article, guilt does seem to be part of the strategy. She writes,

Best possible, ideal, optimal, perfect. Are you the best possible parent? Is your home life ideal? Do you provide optimal meals? Of course not. Those are admirable goals, not minimum standards. Let's rephrase. Is your parenting inadequate? Is your home life subnormal? Do you provide deficient meals? Now it hurts. You may not expect to be far above normal, but you certainly don't want to be below normal. (Wiessinger 2001)

The passage above is an argument that breastfeeding should be the minimal standard; so if one does not breastfeed, one is not an adequate parent. This is very problematic when the United States is one of the only developed nations without paid maternity leave; our government is the largest purchaser of formula; the grocery shelves are full of it; and a generation of people, primarily formula-fed, are here, alive and well, being productive, and happy. It is simply not going to ring true to people to say that formula-use has made people less healthy, whether it is true or not. Smoking was seen as a life or death matter, but most of the women interviewed could not even understand why one would use the term *risky* to describe the use of infant formula in a developed country.

Further, Wiessinger argues that science uses a biological rather than cultural norm; non-smoking and breastfeeding would be the biological norm. Therefore, smoking or feeding formula should both be discussed as increasing risk. Ironically, it was the scientific and medical community that was involved in promoting artificial feeding in the first place, as well as increasing reliance by women on "the experts" and a move toward what Rima Apple calls "scientific mothering" that led to the current situation.

If formula is so risky, why would the FDA allow it on the shelves? My own lactation consultants had to pull out the formula when they discovered my milk was almost gone and my child was not receiving enough calories. To equate it with smoking just does not fit. When women must be rushed into long surgeries after childbirth, their infants are not given human milk from a milk bank, but formula, since the banked milk is saved for premature infants or those who cannot ingest formula. Hospitals are stocked with formula, accept free formula from manufacturers, and are still very frequently giving it to every woman who gives birth. The parallel would be if tobacco companies gave hospitals and doctors free samples to hand out to their patients, and then the doctors shamed people for using them. I realize that the term *risk* is used here in a way that denotes the difference in disease when we go from a biologic norm of breastfeeding to formula, but as I argued in the earlier analysis of AAP documents, it just does not feel correct to people because of the prevalence of formula use.

According to an online article by Lydia Saad appearing on the *Gallup Well Being* page of Gallup.com, on July 24, 2008, even in the 1950s when it seemed everyone smoked, for example, the percentage was actually 44 percent. But in 1972, at the high point of formula use, 78 percent of infants were fed exclusively with formula (Wright 2001). The fact that formula actually did become the norm in practice makes it difficult for people to see it as increasing risks of death, even though they tend to readily accept the idea of the medical benefits of breastfeeding. However, if social conditions more conducive to breastfeeding produced a dramatic increase in the practice and correspondingly, death rates decreased markedly with no other obvious causes, it might be an easier sell.

Increasingly when some raise the issue that the use of risk language is guilt-inducing, some breastfeeding advocates will argue that the feeling is actually regret rather than guilt. Wiessinger, for example, argues that if we help mothers analyze their feelings, it may not be guilt they feel but anger and a sense of being cheated if they were not fully supported and given information. I understand this line of reasoning and agree that women may blame themselves for things rather than being angry at others, even when others are to blame. This assumes that every time a woman does not breast-feed as long as she plans, that someone has failed her. Certainly, this can be the case. This is why I argue for an improved social context for breastfeeding and a right to breastfeed. What if a woman decides not to breastfeed because she is weighing all of the other details of her family's needs and her re-sources? She may decide she must return to work and would rather get back to her infant sooner than find a way to pump three times while away. She may decide to get more sleep and be a more pleasant and happy mother, rather than get up at 4:00 a.m. to pump. She may opt not to breastfeed because of her own mental health or past history of sexual abuse.

These are not crazy hypotheticals, but one only needs to read the gut-wrenching stories of women in these situations on Suzanne Barston's blog, *The Fearless Formula Feeder*. Barston puts it well when she says, "These decisions are never made in a vacuum; some things may be better for the majority but not for the individual" (129). When we look at marginal rates of reduced risk, we are looking at breastfeeding in a vacuum, not at the individ-ual situation of a particular family. Information on breastfeeding should be provided. Programs that support breastfeeding are very important so that women can truly make a choice and not be forced into a choice of formula by circumstance. At the same time, it is important to take the approach of supporting a women's right to breastfeed and provide information about the benefits, while also supporting her decision and recognizing that she is the best person to make decisions about feeding her infant. After all, women have to live in the world that exists now, not the one that we can envision.

Another public health piece that addresses and dismisses the guilt issue is Wight's (2001) article where she says this about doctors being afraid to make women feel guilty about not breastfeeding:

> Breastfeeding is viewed by many as a lifestyle choice rather than a public health issue. Physicians do not hesitate to use guilt to control other parental health choices, such as bicycle helmets, infant car seats, and immunizations. Society views the choice to smoke or not use a car seat as below the accepted standard of child care; parents who make those choices are expected to feel guilty. . . . Guilt is what a human being feels when he or she knowingly chooses a lesser option. Regret is felt when the choices, and the consequences of those choices, are not explained. Ethical caring professionals owe patients accurate information, appropriate guidance, and long-term breastfeeding support. Physicians can help eliminate the regret, but let the guilt fall where it may. (Wight 2001, 337–338)

Many feminists and others are concerned that breastfeeding advocacy fails to take into account the entirety of women's experiences, and the above excerpt is an example. The quote above seems to imply that guilt is appropriate if a woman does not breastfeed, without mentioning any of the real-life situations and cultural norms that may keep her from doing so.

Certainly societal support is necessary and appropriate so that those who wish to breastfeed have a better shot at being successful and not feeling regret about the lost experience. The above passage from Wight equates usage of infant car seats and bike helmets with a process that involves women's considerable time and effort for months or years. The experience varies greatly from woman to woman. Some babies snack all night and their mothers can still get some decent sleep through co-sleeping while others cannot. If the goal is for more women to be able to breastfeed, we need to make it easier to combine with an active public and work life, not equate formula feeding with the act of failing to purchase a bike helmet for $20.00 and making sure it is worn. These types of comparisons to things that require very little work and effort fail to value and recognize the care work women provide when they breastfeed, and they come across as patronizing and condescending.

Not all breastfeeding advocates support using Wight and Wiessinger's approach. Hausman (2012), has argued against *risk* messaging in favor of a women's rights approach, arguing: "Public health achieved many of its most important and life-changing gains in the early twentieth century through broad-based infrastructure changes. The rights framework suggests a return to these priorities, a goal sought by many in public health" (Hausman 2012, 20).

Additionally, some scholars argue that it is in fact shame rather than guilt that many women feel when their best efforts at breastfeeding do not succeed. According to Taylor and Wallace (2012) shame is, "the failure to live up to an ideal, and the understanding of oneself as a lesser creature" (193). After analyzing parenting message boards, they find that many of the women describe themselves as failures or bad mothers. They argue, "Guilt, then, is a response to what one does, while shame is a response to who one is" (198). Another problem with advocacy that induces shame is that it is likely to result in inaction rather than action to make amends, as with the response of guilt to a specific act or wrongdoing that has done harm. Taylor and Wallace argue for a feminist breastfeeding advocacy that puts mothers at the center, listens to their concerns and experiences, and understands the challenges they face (Taylor and Wallace 2012).

Jacqueline Wolf (2003) writing in *The Journal of Public Health* compares the current campaign to increase breastfeeding exclusivity and duration to the public health movement of the turn of the century. She writes:

> The first sentence of the HHS piece—"Breastfeeding is one of the most important contributors to infant health"—is reminiscent of the early-twentieth century public health campaigns' insistence that having been breastfed was the single most powerful predictor of an infant's ability to survive childhood.

I think it is important to point out some differences between the two time-periods. In the early twentieth century, diarrhea, often caused by unpasteurized cow's milk, was the leading cause of infant death. There is a difference between an infant not surviving the first year due to diarrhea and the current situation of formula-fed babies having higher rates of ear infections and other diseases. As Barston (2012) points out, in the developed countries where water supplies are generally safe, use of bottles and formula is not typically life-threatening. Also, the earlier crisis involved contaminated milk not pasteurized at home or properly stored, coupled with the problem of cow's milk being inappropriate for infants. Formula was developed to modify milk for infants (even though it is not as good as breast milk); it is not causing death from diarrhea in high rates in developed countries.

As Wolf (2008) describes, the early 1900s campaign focused on educating parents about the dangers of not breastfeeding. If the public health goal today is to increase breastfeeding rates, this approach seems limited. The biggest difference is a generation of formula-use that was not present during the last campaign. There is also an increase in women in the workplace and the media image of the sexualized breast, which Kedrowski and Lipscomb (2008) and others point out (Blum 1999; Carter 1995). Another important challenge is that breastfeeding in public was not something that was a common everyday practice in American culture at the turn of the twentieth century (colonial times were less restrictive) though breastfeeding itself was. Women are now more fully incorporated into public life and until the public space is accommodating, formula is going to be attractive to many women because if they breastfeed, cultural norms may force them to dramatically alter their lifestyle to spend much more time out of the public space.

The approach of discussing the dangers of formula just is not going to be effective in the same way that discussing the dangers of cow's milk may have worked at the turn of the twentieth century. The fact that formula feeding was encouraged by many in the medical community, but now is being called dangerous, creates a major credibility problem that needs to be addressed. The U.S. government also has a credibility problem when its health officials use this language since the federal government is the major purchaser of infant formula in the United States (Oliveira, Frazão and Smallwood 2011). Also, at the turn of the twentieth century when doctors had begun to get involved in supervising infant feeding, the issue of hospital practices (which the AAP still critiques in its 2012 breastfeeding statement) was not a major challenge as most births took place in the home (Apple 1987).

The best approach to getting more women to follow the AAP guidelines probably has little to do with education of mothers themselves (who generally know the benefits to infants and themselves) but should focus on the broader public and on making breastfeeding more feasible for working mothers. For each person I interviewed, whether she was a mother, breastfeeding advocate, or medical professional, I asked why they thought most women did not breastfeed for the duration recommended by the AAP. Each and every one of them answered that the women probably had to go back to work. Even those women who followed the AAP recommendation on breastfeeding duration and worked cited this reason. They, more than anyone, knew the personal costs and challenges involved with combining working, pumping, and breastfeeding.

Rather than continuing with education policies that focus narrowly on women and tweaking wording from *breast is best* to *formula is risky* in an attempt to get women to breastfeed longer, advocates should focus on the debate about the inadequacy of the Family and Medical Leave Act of 1993. To its credit, the United States Breastfeeding Committee (USBC) does list working for paid family leave as a goal of the organization, which was part of its five-year strategic plan from 2009 to 2013. The USBC's Activities included taking part in a work-family coalition convened by the National Partnership for Women and Families, and outreach to state breastfeeding coalitions to support federal- and state-paid family leave (USBC 2013).

Education campaigns are inexpensive compared with policies that help address the realities of family, work, and caregiving. I spoke with several breastfeeding advocates about banning formula or making it available only by prescription; most indicated that while they had supported that policy in the past or would like to in their heart of hearts, they felt it would not be the right policy at this time. Most indicated that they feared that people would feed even less appropriate foods instead, recognizing that some face challenges because they have to return to work early for financial reasons or rely on family members who do not support breastfeeding for child-care assistance.

Another problematic aspect of the 2012 AAP policy statement from the Section on Breastfeeding is that while it does go on to address various barriers to breastfeeding, including hospital practices and how they can be overcome (834–837), the abstract opens with a statement that could be seen as not fully recognizing the many complex factors that conspire to make breastfeeding difficult in the United States for many women. The 2012 policy statement abstract opens this way:

> Breastfeeding and human milk are the normative standards for infant feeding and nutrition. Given the documented short- and long-term medical and neuro-developmental advantages of breastfeeding, infant nutrition should be considered a *public health issue and not only a lifestyle choice*. The American Academy of Pediatrics reaffirms its recommendation of exclusive breastfeeding for about 6 months, followed by continued breastfeeding as complementary foods are introduced, with continuation of breastfeeding for one year or longer as mutually desired by mother and infant. (AAP 2012; italics added)

The use of the phrase *lifestyle choice* is new compared to the previous two statements. While it is understandable that the Section on Breastfeeding of the AAP would frame breastfeeding as a public health issue, this particular language right up front and center in the abstract puts the focus on individual women's choices, rather than medical and societal choices that have help lead the way to lower breastfeeding rates during the mid-twentieth century in the first place. The phrase seems too close to the language used by some physicians in the past who chided women who did not breastfeed for being lazy or concerned with frivolous matters (Apple 1987). A more collective and cooperative tone could go a long way since other pediatricians, who are not part of the Section on Breastfeeding, may be less inclined to buy into the statement if they see it as trivializing real barriers to breastfeeding that require a wide-ranging effort to remedy.

In terms of substantive changes in the presentation of the medical evidence for recommending breastfeeding, there is some attention to methodological issues pointed out by Barston (2012) and Wolf (2011) since the release of the previous policy statement in 2005. Some critiques are that the causal mechanism that leads to better outcomes for infants fed breast milk is not always explained well, sample sizes can be small, and the extent of controls used for factors related to both parents and socioeconomic status are frequently unclear (Barston 2012). Since the definition used for breastfeeding often includes infants fed at the breast and infants fed pumped breast milk in a bottle or other feeding device, it may not always be known whether benefits accrue due to the properties of the milk itself or due to other factors related to the act of putting the baby to the breast (AAP 2012; Barston 2012). The AAP 2012 statement itself recognizes limitations and says this:

> Major methodologic issues have been raised as to the quality of some of these studies, especially as to the size of the study populations, quality of the data set, inadequate adjustment for confounders, absence of distinguishing between "any" or "exclusive" breastfeeding, and lack of a defined causal relationship between breastfeeding and the specific outcome. In addition, there are inherent practical and ethical issues that have precluded prospective randomized interventional trials of different feeding regimens. (e828)

The document then goes on to cite studies that do indicate causal mechanisms, to the extent they are known, and to indicate when cofounders or controls are accounted for in the studies (though they are not enumerated specifically in the statement). This attempt to address critiques of the medical evidence, demonstrates an important exchange that is an integral part of the academic peer review process. It is what makes science accountable and open to peer scrutiny. This stands in contrast to the rather ideological tone that the abstracts of the statements have moved toward from the 1997 document to the 2012 document. The science can speak for itself and allow informed choices; women do not need to have their infant-feeding decisions, made within the many constraints of their lives, belittled with the phrase *lifestyle choices*. Their pediatricians, who are not members of the Breastfeeding Section of the AAP, may not be swayed by it either. Declaring breastfeeding the normative standard will not make women breastfeed; but methodologically sound evidence combined with policies and resources that make it possible without requiring some women to go to "heroic efforts," as Hausman (2012) puts it, might increase breastfeeding rates.

Putting the Public Back in Public Health: From Behavior to Policy

While the 2012 AAP statement rightly recognizes constraints to breastfeeding and gives recommendations on how physicians, women, and businesses can work together to improve public health through breastfeeding, the document fails to mention the option of paid family leave and also leaves out the costs of breastfeeding in terms of women's time and effort when it calculates the cost-benefit analysis for breastfeeding. This does not mean the case cannot and should not be made for breastfeeding, only that all of the costs must be included. Feminists have long pointed out that the unpaid care work women do becomes invisible and allows inequity to continue (Waring 1990; Tronto 2013; Hochschild 2003). Recognizing this work (pumping basically becoming a third shift for women) does not mean one is anti-breastfeeding, but calls attention to the real reasons some women may not breastfeed even if they have access to pumping breaks and beautiful facilities in which to do it (Barston 2010).

Countries with paid family leave have higher rates of breastfeeding. Many of the programs correspond quite well with the period of time recommended by the AAP for breastfeeding (six months exclusively and then at least another six months with complimentary solid foods), yet these policies are never mentioned in the document as a model for the United States (Ray 2008; OECD 2014). While one may say the document is aimed at physicians and does not get into public policy, it does include a lengthy section on the "business case for breastfeeding," which focuses mostly on employers investing in their employees by providing pumping facilities. It also discusses the provisions of the Affordable Care Act and what they mean for employees. For example, this section states, "The return on investment has been calculated that for every $1 invested in creating and supporting a lactation support program (including a designated pump site that guarantees privacy, availability of refrigeration, and a hand-washing facility, and appropriate mother break-time), there is a $2 to $3 dollar return" (AAP 2012, e836).

The attention to pumping is important since not all breastfeeding women will want or be able to take long family leaves even if they were paid. But as Blum (1999) and others point out, pumping expressed milk to feed to infants is not the same as the embodied experience of breastfeeding, and could create a double-edge sword where women become *supermoms* who are working, managing the household, and expressing breast milk for their babies (Barston 2012). The aid of technology can still basically allow them to enter the workforce "as men," with a much more modest modification than paid leave, which could prove to be more beneficial for the well-being of both women and infants (Blum 1999).

If the AAP truly wants to make breastfeeding possible for more women, it might investigate the return on investment for paid family leave, as they did for lactation support programs. This would be something the AAP statement could appropriately include that fits well with the framework on breastfeeding as a public health issue. Three states already have paid family leave funded by employee contributions. President Obama has come out in favor of some form of paid family leave, and proposed legislation in Congress creating a national policy has eighty-eight co-sponsors in the House of Representatives (Goldfarb 2014).

Additionally, as part of its section on "the business case" for supporting breastfeeding, it could recommend voluntary benefits from employers to invest in their workers by developing on-site day care, company paid leave benefits or programs such as those of the Parenting in the Workplace Institute (PIWI). PIWI develops programs that allow some workers to bring their infants to work with them when they are young. Some research has shown a variety of benefits to the employers in terms of retention, recruiting, and lower health insurance costs (PIWI 2014).

While the AAP statements on breastfeeding did not include recommendations for paid family leave to help increase breastfeeding rates, this idea was included in a presentation entitled, "Breastfeeding as a public health issue and how the AAP supports the use of human milk," given at the 2013 More Than Latch conference in Chesapeake Virginia. The speaker, Dr. Natasha K. Sriraman, is an assistant professor of pediatrics at Eastern Virginia Medical School, as well as an International Board Certified Lactation Consultant (IBCLC), who also has a master's of public health (MPH). Her daughter accompanied her to the conference, and Dr. Sriraman explained that she was breastfed for a year. Her combination of credentials position her well to support breastfeeding as well as advocate for broader societal support for breastfeeding as a public health issue.

Dr. Sriraman pointed out that the United States is among five countries out of 173 that do not have paid maternity leave. She explained that the United States is in the company of Lesotho, Liberia, Swaziland, and Papua New Guinea when it comes to family or maternity leave policies. Additionally, she indicated that 98 out of 168 countries give new mothers fourteen weeks of paid leave or more (Sriraman 2013). The attention given to this issue by a pediatrician is encouraging because it goes beyond the model of focusing on individual behavior to look at how public policies can affect behavior and public health.

The percentage of female pediatricians is increasing, with females making up 69 percent of all residents in 2004 to 2005. Also, more female pediatricians than men saw themselves increasing their involvement in children's community health issues (Solomon et al. 2006). While this article did not focus specifically on breastfeeding support, the trends identified may cause a positive change in terms of more extensive pediatrician support of breastfeeding in the rank and file membership of the AAP, as well as more extensive expertise in lactation and support for broader societal initiatives to support breastfeeding through family leave, workplace pumping, and child care policies as is exemplified by Dr. Sririman's advocacy of these policies.

An IBCLC and WIC employee whom I met at the LATCH conference where Sririman spoke explained, "Now we have doctors who are specializing in breastfeeding medicine. They're still a very small percentage, but we have the Academy of Breastfeeding Medicine and doctors are getting involved with that. Many, many of those physicians are also becoming IBCLCs and getting certified."

On the other hand, she said that some physicians just are not as concerned about breastfeeding. For example, she explained how one client has an infant with the condition *tongue-tie*, which makes it difficult for the infant to latch on to the breast. She is pumping and bottle feeding but would like to breastfeed. She explained, "Her pediatrician dismissed it. 'You're making enough milk for the baby. That's all you need to worry about.' He didn't care that she couldn't put the baby to the breast."

Indeed, when I asked another IBCLC and WIC employee in another county about some of the biggest challenges she sees with supporting women who want to breastfeed, she stated that many pediatricians in her area did not seem to understand breastfeeding. Breastfed babies have looser mustard colored stools, but many of her clients were never told this and thought it was diarrhea. She related that a familiar refrain from clients was, "I went to the pediatrician. He said, 'it's a reaction to your milk.'"

She also mentioned that if there were any weight gain issues at all, the pediatricians were quick "for me to take the baby off the breast immediately." This contrasts with the procedure for determining if supplementation is medically necessary, which is to weigh the child, put the child to the breast for a feeding, and then weigh the child again. If the child is not receiving a full feed, supplementation is done using techniques that help maintain milk supply and breastfeeding. The child is also checked for signs of dehydration, and parents keep a log of wet diapers (Neifert 2001). IBCLCs are trained in all of these procedures, so pediatricians with this credential or who employ IBCLCs directly are in the best position to support breastfeeding women. The WIC employee who shared these stories felt that building more support from pediatricians was one of the most important challenges for supporting breastfeeding in her county.

The Second Paradox: Quality Formula Feeding and Access to Formula

A public health approach to infant feeding and nutrition should also focus on improving formula, not just increasing breastfeeding; even if formula cannot come close to human milk, it is used by hospitals, with milk banks being reserved only for the sickest of infants. Even if only those with contraindications for breastfeeding used formula, there would still be a large number of infants requiring formula due to various contraindications. While the AAP downplays contraindications for breastfeeding (AAP 2012), according to the New York Department of Health's *Breastfeeding Pocket Guide for Health Care Providers* from July 2010, those advised not to breastfeed are those who:

- Are infected with HIV
- Are infected with HTLV (Human T-cell Lymphotropic Virus) Type I or II
- Use illegal drugs
- Are taking cancer chemotherapy agents that interfere with DNA replication and cell division

- Are receiving Radiation Therapies; however, Nuclear Medicine Therapies only require breastfeeding to be interrupted temporarily
- Have active herpes lesions on the breast (shingles, chicken pox)
- Have an infant who has galactosemia
- Have untreated, active TB (New York Department of Health 2010).

Since infants affected by the above list will most likely be given formula, we should all be very concerned with how those children can also get excellent nutrition by further improvements in formula or increased access to milk banks. These contraindications mean many infants will not be breastfed no matter how many ads depicting the risks of formula are run, which makes focusing child nutrition advocacy only on breastfeeding problematic.

The goal should be the best possible support for breastfeeding and the best possible substitutes for situations in which children are not breastfed. Increasing the number of and access to milk banks is another solution that would enable those children who are not breastfed to access the antibodies present in breast milk.

Response of Women's groups to Public Health Initiatives and the AAP

While academic feminist and other scholars have written in support or opposition to government and medical advocacy of breastfeeding, the National Organization for Women (NOW) has also taken positions on breastfeeding advocacy and policy. A search of NOW's national website in March of 2008 showed twenty-three articles on breastfeeding posted on the site or appearing in the National NOW Times. The articles or documents ranged from 1998–2007. In another search in 2015, I found four additional articles since 2007 posted between 2011 and 2013.

In 1998, the organization responded to AAP recommendations of exclusive breastfeeding in the first six months and continued breastfeeding with solid foods until one year, by calling for societal and employer support of nursing mothers. They called for many of the same policy changes in welfare-to-work and family leave policy they continue to support today, most of which have not been realized. The summer issue of the 1998 National NOW Times reported the following:

> I nursed both of my daughters, and it was possible because I work for an employer that made it possible, said NOW Executive Vice President Kim Gandy. But most employers don't provide those resources, and some actively take steps that make breastfeeding impossible for their employees. (NOW 1998)

And also:

As a mother of two myself, I am excited by the progress that our society is making in its attitude toward breastfeeding, said NOW Action V.P. Elizabeth Toledo. In my birthing class, when I was pregnant with my first child, I was the only person whose mother had breastfed her children. Things have clearly changed, but as with so many other issues, we still have more work to do to gain greater public acceptance and proper access for mothers. (NOW 1998)

Most of the NOW articles on the national website emphasized the need for more societal and employer support of breastfeeding. A major theme was the sexualization of the breast, leading to a lack of support for public breastfeeding. One article discusses the Kansas bill and the involvement of Amy Swan in lobbying members of the legislature on this issue (Afriyle 2006). This same article discusses the other legislative efforts of NOW in the support of parents and families, as well as the other changes necessary to support breastfeeding:

Breastfeeding in private is a luxury not afforded to women who live with large families, work at places that do not have private facilities to pump, or for women who must travel with their newborns on public transportation. . . . Effecting change through legislation is half the battle. Even after NOW wins the fight for paid family leave, women-friendly workplaces, and increased funding of programs for low-income mothers, many babies will not benefit from the nutrients in breast milk unless their mothers feel comfortable and secure in breastfeeding. The encouragement of family, the support of friends, and public acceptance can make our world a healthier place for babies. . . . Pending legislation in Congress needs your support too. S.Res.403, introduced in March, calls on states to recognize the benefits of breastfeeding by implementing programs and acknowledges the economic and social benefits of supporting mothers in breastfeeding. H.R. 2122, introduced in May of 2005, provides tax incentives for breastfeeding mothers and holds all breast pumps to a gold standard of performance. Although neither is likely to pass in this Congress, we look forward to starting anew with a House and Senate that will be more sensitive to our concerns, and more women-friendly. (Afriyle 2006)

The legislation referred to here was not passed, but the Affordable Care Act of 2010 contained provisions requiring employers (with over fifty employees) to allow hourly employees non-paid break time to pump in a private place that is not a bathroom. It is clear that in its support of the opportunity to breastfeed, NOW is taking an approach that focuses on the barriers to breastfeeding, rather than an approach that takes the social environment as a given, and then tries to go from there, with attempts to modify individual behavior. For example, NOW documents show that the organization has not supported government education efforts that use language that focuses on the risks of formula. This position can be seen in an open letter to the Secretary of Health and Human Services regarding the National Breastfeeding Awareness Campaign (NBAC) ads that first ran in June of 2004: "Recent commercials produced by the Department of Health and Human Services (HHS) accuse women who don't breastfeed their newborns exclusively for six months of irresponsible parenting" (Gandy 2006).

The harsh commercials ignore the real barriers for women who want to breastfeed Gandy continued:

> Equating a woman's decision not to breastfeed with log rolling or mechanical bull riding while pregnant insults the millions of women who are physically unable to breastfeed, are advised not to breastfeed due to illness and medical treatment, or are unable to breastfeed for six months because of inadequate workplace accommodations. The National Organization for Women wants all women to have the opportunity to breastfeed their babies. According to medical experts and public health officials, the nutrients in breast milk provide infants with antibodies that help protect them against infection and potentially against chronic diseases. Yet, according to a 2003 Centers for Disease Control study, 86 percent of mothers do not breastfeed exclusively for six months, and these barriers are part of the reason. (Gandy 2006)

The letter goes on to list all of the actions that the HHS can take to help increase the numbers of women who breastfeed exclusively for six months by issuing recommendations to employers and government outlining the best practices for accommodating breastfeeding mothers. These include: extending nutritional supplements for new mothers under the WIC program, recommending that Congress clarify the law regarding public breastfeeding, and amending welfare-to-work requirements to allow nursing mothers to delay seeking employment until they have stopped breastfeeding (Gandy 2006).

The letter is interesting in that it voices support for breastfeeding, yet recognizes the reasons why all women do not breastfeed. This differs from much advocacy in that it recognizes the social context in which decisions regarding infant feeding are made. Also, the NOW focus is broader in terms of legislation. While the AAP has focused primarily on workplace accommodations for pumping, NOW has reflected the feminist concern for lack of opportunity for women of lower socioeconomic status to breastfeed by recommending broader policy changes at the federal level that include changes to the work requirements of the TANF (Temporary Aid to Needy Families) program. The USBC does advocate for paid family leave in addition to workplace support and protection of public breastfeeding (USBC 2013). This approach combines an individual rights approach and a social responsibility approach which provides the best opportunity for women to actually be able to exercise their right to breastfeed.

Research on Effects of Public Health Approaches

Public health studies explore which types of support have been most important in women's decisions to breastfeed. An article by Reeves et al (2006) in
the *Florida Public Health Review* surveyed breastfeeding mothers across
ethnic and racial groups in six northern Florida counties. One major finding
was that most of the women reported that they did not wean due to a lack of
support, but because of the need to return to work or school. Only 27.6
percent reported that there was a convenient place to pump at work or school,
so the weaning finding is not surprising. The women also responded that they
did receive support from their husbands, but that they could use more support. Further, the respondents reported that while support was important to
them, the decision was ultimately their own. A strong majority reported they
would breastfeed future children. While 48 percent responded that they
strongly agreed that it should be recommended that all women breastfeed,
only 38 percent agreed that all women should breastfeed. The authors reported a strong sense among respondents that a woman should make her own
decision regarding whether or not to breastfeed (Reeves 2006).

The conclusions of the study recommended more social support and further support from spouses (Reeves et al. 2006). There was no recommendation for increased school and workplace support through pumping facilities,
on-site day care, or longer and paid parental leave. This is surprising given
that this was the most frequently reported reason for weaning. In fact, work
was more commonly mentioned than the age of the child or his or her ability
to eat solid foods. Further research in the field of public health might build on
this study to see if the findings apply to other regions.

Also, future studies could explore the type of support women are seeking
from spouses, given that many already reported that their spouses were supportive of their decision to breastfeed. Perhaps women are thinking of more
assistance with other household tasks rather than just moral support and a
shared priority on the importance of breastfeeding. Rippeyoung and Noonan
(2012) find a link between breastfeeding and women doing more of all of the
work in caring for children. To address this "dark side of breastfeeding" they
advance a *feminist advocacy* approach. This approach neither downplays the
division-of-labor problem as short-term, nor uses it as a reason not to advocate breastfeeding, but instead urges that breastfeeding advocacy give greater
attention to fathers, employers, and the social structure.

Public Health Approaches Informed by Feminism

Anthropologist and breastfeeding advocate Penny Van Esterik (1995) has
said, "Advocacy on behalf of breastfeeding is incomplete and probably ineffective unless accompanied by a politically informed analysis of the obsta-

cles to breastfeeding" (145). After reviewing the major public health approaches to breastfeeding advocacy, the arguments of Boswell-Penc (2006) and, others advocating for more feminist engagement with the subject of breastfeeding, become even clearer. Hausman (2012) and Taylor and Wallace (2012) demonstrate that critiques of the approaches used in breastfeeding advocacy can be made by feminists without rejecting advocacy altogether. The problems occur when public health promotions focus too much attention on individual behavior, instead of the lack of infrastructure to support breastfeeding. This gives all the more reason for feminists to engage with those in public health in order to offer insights into approaches that are likely to be the most effective not in "getting women to breastfeed" but in making sure that every woman has the opportunity to do so and can do so in a supportive environment.

The Breastfeeding and Feminism International Conference, which has been held each year since 2005, is making progress in bringing feminist input into public health approaches to breastfeeding advocacy. It is cohosted by the Center for Women's Health and Wellness at the University of North Carolina at Greensboro (UNCG) and the Carolina Global Breastfeeding Institute at UNC Chapel Hill. The Social-Ecological Model (SEM) of public health advanced by Smith, Hausman and Labbok (2012) in their edited book based on the proceedings of the 2010 symposium offers much promise because it focuses on how social factors affect health and disease and opens up the possibility of a greater emphasis on removing obstacles that prevent women from having the opportunity to breastfeed. This is certainly a step in the right direction and a model for a type of public health and medical advocacy that has the potential to lead to the transformed social context for breastfeeding so many scholars have advocated (Blum 1999; Carter 1995; Kedrowski and Lipscomb 2008).

NOTES

1. See discussion in chapter 3.

Chapter Six

Breasts, Bottles, and Maternal Activism

Brittany Warfield sat outside of a Hollister clothing store in a Houston, Texas mall nursing her infant in late December 2012, when she was chastised and asked to leave by the store manager. An article posted online for MY FOX.com, KDFW Channel 4, by Demali Keith on December 27, 2012, recounted, "The manager demanded she leave the store. Warfield said he was yelling, 'You have to go. You have to get up and go now. You're out here doing this. You have to go. We don't have this set up for you to do that here.'"

A post from January 3, 2013, by Dionna Ford on the website Best for Babes, entitled "Racy Hollister Okay with Sexy Pics, Not Breastfeeding, for Tweens," shows a photograph of a Hollister ad in which a bikini clad girl and half-dressed boy are locked in an embrace. Ford points out an irony many see when those who appear to profit from the breast as a sex object express discomfort with breastfeeding, even when the nursing mother is using a cover, as was the case with Warfield. Women rallied to support Warfield online, and a nurse-in was scheduled for January 5, 2013 at Hollister stores nationwide. Most nurse-ins went off without confrontation, with the exception of a conflict involving security guards and police in Concord Mall in Delaware. Delaware has a public breastfeeding law. The state where Warfield was approached, Texas, also has a law protecting the right to breastfeed anywhere women otherwise have a right to be.

Public Breastfeeding Activism

As illustrated above, some breastfeeding women and their supporters have used the technique known as the nurse-in as a way to draw attention to the issue of breastfeeding in public. The practice gets its name from the direct-action technique of a sit-in—breastfeeding women, their family members, and supporters occupy a public place where a woman has been asked not to breastfeed and they breastfeed their infants there. In doing so, they protest the attempts to exclude them from the public space. This is similar in tactic to the sit-in used across the south during the civil rights movement between 1960 and 1962 following a "trigger incident" on February 1, 1960, in Greensboro, North Carolina (Laue 1989).

In some cases, nurse-ins are used to bring attention to an existing state law or to help rally support for a law clarifying the right to breastfeed. One difference from the sit-in movement in the 1960s is that the nurse-ins are protesting a policy or practice on the part of business owners or employees rather than laws that directly exclude breastfeeding women. Thus, the risks to participants are lower in that they are not typically arrested for their participation.

However, the Concord Mall nurse-in in Delaware did involve police being called to the location by security guards. When the participating women showed a copy of the Delaware law that protects breastfeeding to the officers, they let the women go (Ford 2013). Another difference is that while nurse-ins are typically held on one day in multiple locations of the same business after a trigger incident involving a woman breastfeeding, they are not typically held day-after-day in the same location as in the lunch counter sit-ins of the civil rights movement (Laue 1989).

Nurse-ins are often organized online in response to a breastfeeding woman being asked to leave an establishment or to use the restroom to breastfeed her infant. According to a December 29, 2011, online column, *Family Matters* by Bonnie Rochman, the nurse-in at Target Stores was coordinated on a Facebook page and took place on December 28, 2011, in two hundred fifty stores across the nation in thirty-five states. According to Rochman, it was organized in response to a Houston woman (discreetly breastfeeding her five-month old in a remote section of the store) being asked by Target employees to move to a private dressing room, despite a state law protecting her right to breastfeed.

Often media and social media accounts of the nurse-in activities that I analyzed placed nurse-ins within the broader breastfeeding advocacy or lactivist movement associated with La Leche League (LLL) and other organized groups that promote and support breastfeeding. However, my analysis shows that most participants involved in nurse-ins have been from much more diffuse groups of mothers and interested people organized by social media. Many of the families involved have not been involved in breastfeeding advocacy or any type of activism before.

The nurse-ins share some similarities to the sputtering interests explored by Laura Woliver (1993) in, *From Outrage to Action: The Politics of Grass-Roots Dissent*. However, social media and the rise of Internet parenting websites and blogs have added another dimension to previous categorizations of either grass-roots activism or "checkbook affiliates." In the latter, one simply devotes money to a cause without direct action (Woliver 1993, 4). The nurse-ins are triggered in response to a specific incident; but once they are over for a particular date, they don't tend to be repeated in the same place on a regular basis. However, there is often a continued discussion of the incidents and nurse-ins on social media and parenting websites.

Use of the direct-action techniques common in social movements is not completely new in the area of breastfeeding advocacy. The Infant Formula Action Coalition (IFAC) launched a boycott of Nestlé to protest aggressive marketing techniques in developing countries. The Nestlé Boycott began in 1977 and was suspended in 1984 when Nestlé adopted the World Health Organization (WHO) International Code of Marketing Baby Milk Substitutes. However, a boycott was re-launched by organizations in the United Kingdom and continues today due to allegations that the company is not following the WHO code (created to regulate the marketing of formula in 1981). The boycott has been called one of the most successful boycotts in history (Van Esterik 1989; Krasny 2012).

More broadly, it is not uncommon for women to organize and be involved in social movements geared toward what they perceive as the best interests of children. Scholars have documented modern mothers' movements and have observed that those involved do not necessarily identify as feminists. Nathanson (2008) argues they are doing feminist work nonetheless because, "Maternal activism is an explicit example of the personal made political" (253). This chapter explores how women have come together to challenge cultural notions about what is appropriate in the public space, change corporate policy, and effect legal change. While sometimes breastfeeding advocacy groups support the events and sometimes self-described feminists are involved, for the most part the women organize as mothers and their families and not as part of either of these movements.

I reviewed news articles and readers' comments reporting on those involved in this kind of breastfeeding rights activism to gain some insight on the involvement and the responses it garners. In all of the nurse-in events that I analyzed, there were some common themes. The incidents involved an array of women: some white, some women of color, some working outside the home and some not, some activists for other causes and some not, some using a cover when confronted and some not. A common theme raised by participants, as reported in the news stories, was frustration or anger at having been shamed for doing something that is so widely promoted as healthy for babies and women. They also expressed frustration with the sexual breast being accepted in public, often barely covered, while the lactating breast was met with disgust even when all or most of the beast was covered by the baby or a cover (Ford 2013; Lewin 2005; Leckie 2010; Rochman 2011; Afriyle 2006).

Ironically, many of the incidents occurred in states that had already adopted public breastfeeding laws. The stories described above show the problems that can occur when owners of public accommodations are not aware that the laws even exist. On the other hand, I also found in my interviews with women who had breastfed, that many of them were not aware of the laws either. For example, Danielle said, "I had no idea there was a law and I just assumed I could feed her wherever I wanted."

In one case, activism prompted a new state law. According to a story by Adrianne Mand Lewin, appearing on ABCNews.com, on December 20, 2005, Lori Rueger was shopping near a Victoria's Secret store in Mount Pleasant, South Carolina, when her baby became hungry and started to cry. She asked if she could nurse her child in the dressing room and the clerk suggested she might be more comfortable in a nearby public restroom. When Rueger expressed dissatisfaction with the idea of feeding her child in a public restroom, she was asked to leave the store.

When she told others what happened, they organized a nurse-in outside the store to bring attention to the issue of breastfeeding in public. A group of the mothers formed a committee to lobby the state legislature for legislation protecting breastfeeding in public. On February 14, 2006, the South Carolina House of Representatives passed a bill protecting the right to breastfeed in public, without the need for floor debate, and sent the bill on to the Senate. The legislation was signed into law on May 2, 2006. According to the ABC article, Reuger denied being a lactivist. When asked about her role in getting the legislation passed, she said, "I'm just a mom who was trying to feed her baby the only way that she can eat and a lot happened because of that" (Lewin 2005).

In Maryland, on the other hand, legislation protecting public breastfeeding has been in effect since 2003. Despite this legislation, Lorig Charkoudian was asked to use the restroom to breastfeed in a Starbucks store in Silver Spring, Maryland in August of 2004. In response to this experience, she organized a nurse-in at the store and launched a national letter-writing campaign to try to persuade the company to adopt a national policy allowing breastfeeding in Starbucks. The letter, which was posted on Charkoudian's website, is written in the nursing child's voice and is addressed to the CEO of Starbucks at the time, Orin C. Smith (See Appendix A).[1] The company responded that it will instruct its managers and employees to follow the law in Maryland and in other states and localities where the stores are located. However, despite the promise to have employees follow the state laws, a similar incident occurred in Louisiana in 2005 in violation of Louisiana's public breastfeeding law, which was adopted in 2001.

According to an article entitled, "Coffee and Milk" in the *Pomona College Magazine*, Spring 2006 issue, Charkoudian explained, "When you respond to breastfeeding as though it's shameful and needs to be hidden, that's going to decrease the amount of breastfeeding. The less people see it, the less common it is, and the less people will do it." The Starbucks policy of leaving decisions on public breastfeeding (in the absence of a state law protecting it) up to store managers was still in effect at this writing. In one widely reported Canadian incident, however, the manager took the side of the breastfeeding customer when another customer complained. In this case, a Toronto Starbucks employee responded to a customer who called breastfeeding "disgusting" by giving the breastfeeding mother a refill on her coffee and apologizing to her for the customer's loud complaining (Wykes 2014).

It is clear that Charkoudian sees her activism on public breastfeeding as empowering women and mothers. In an interview with Jackie Regales at the website Hip Mamma in 2005 she said:

> Yes, definitely. I've been reading Shannon Malamud Smith's book, *A Potent Spell*, recently, and it's all about how our connection to and immense love for our children inherently is a fear of harm coming to them, which has historically been used to control women. You know, it's that whole idea of 'We want you to stay home, be a good mother, raise your children correctly, and keep them safe.' It's very threatening to a lot of people to bring motherhood out into the public arena and women are subject to these intense feelings of shame and embarrassment when they are recognized as transgressing those boundaries.

Many scholars have long argued that motherhood and the care work mothers do needs to be valued in a way that goes beyond romanticism to include actual material and cultural support (Kittay 1999; Tronto 2013; Woliver 2002). Challenging the status quo and bringing the full range of mothering, which includes breastfeeding for many women, out into the public realm must certainly be considered a women's rights issue.

Despite the law in Maryland and earlier efforts to normalize public breastfeeding there, another nurse-in was held five summers later. This story is told in a June 6, 2010 article by Katie Leckie entitled, "Nursing Mothers Unite at FSK Mall" in the *Frederick News-Post*. It relates how Anne-Marie Luciano, an anti-trust lawyer in Washington, DC, was nursing her daughter in the FSK mall, near the children's play area, when she was approached by a woman and a security guard and was asked to move to the nursing room. She knew the law in Maryland and stayed where she was. She organized a nurse-in two weeks later to help bring awareness to the 2003 Maryland law that states that a woman has a right to nurse her child on public or private property where she otherwise has a right to be. Luciano told the *Frederick News-Post*, "This has accomplished what I set out to do." She continued, "to raise awareness to the issue and to make women feel empowered to feed their babies as they choose."

The story of Amy Swan illustrates the involvement of many wide-ranging groups in support of breastfeeding rights and the familiar conflicts that arose when they engaged in activism to fight the harassment of breastfeeding women in public accommodations in Kansas.

The Case of the Kansas Breastfeeding Rights Law

Kansas House Bill 2284 clarified that women have the right to breastfeed their infants anywhere that they have a right to be, and also allowed them to be exempt from jury duty. The bill was introduced by the House Committee on Health and Human Services at the request of Representative Paul Davis in 2006. The National Organization for Women's (NOW) national on-line newsletter reported that breastfeeding mother Amy Swan of Lawrence, Kansas, had lobbied for the law after she had been asked not to breastfeed her infant daughter in the nursery of a health club by a male who did not want his son to see a nursing mother. When she contacted the owner of the club, he shamed her for nursing in front of a man she did not know and asked her why she did not consider others' feelings when she chose to nurse her daughter. He recommended Swan go into a restroom and shut the door (Afriyle 2006).

The bill was first introduced in 2005 when hearings were held in the Senate Public Health and Welfare Committee on March 14. Representative Stephanie Sharp testified on behalf of the legislation in addition to six other speakers. At least fifteen letters in support of HB 2284 were also sent to the House of Representatives in February 2005 from LLL leaders and members, as well as other members of the community (See Appendix B).

The bill passed the House in 2005, but was, at first, amended to include the word "discreetly." Some were concerned that women would expose too much of their breasts while nursing in public. LLL advocates argued for removing this provision due to its subjectivity and because it could be used against breastfeeding women. Ultimately, the bill was amended by the Senate Committee on Public Health and Welfare to delete "discreetly" from the final version of the bill that passed both chambers in the 2006 session. It was signed into law by Governor Kathleen Sebelius on March 6, 2006.

Testimony in support of HB 2284 was given in both 2005 and 2006 before the Senate Public Health and Welfare Committee. Additional testimony in support of HB 2284 was also submitted by nursing mothers, nurses, members of the KAW Breastfeeding Coalition, lactation consultants, LLL members, a physician from a local hospital, a representative of the Greater Kansas Chapter (Topeka Division) of The March of Dimes, and an official from the Kansas Department of Health and Environment. Interestingly, although the bill did not pass until 2006, the only public testimony in opposition to the bill in 2005 was from a representative from the Kansas Office of Judicial Registration, opposing the jury duty provision. The testimony can be divided into three groups of supporters: the medical community (including public health officials, nurses, and physicians), breastfeeding advocates (La Leche League leaders, the KAW Breastfeeding Coalition, and Lactation Consultants), and individual nursing mothers and their families (See Appendixes B and C).

Several themes were found to be present across the testimony for both years: In Support

- Health benefits of breastfeeding to the infant and mother
- Need for societal support of nursing mothers
- Contributions of breastfeeding to overall public health
- Rights of women and infants

In opposition (The only opposition was to the jury duty exemption.):

- The state requires a strong jury pool.
- Discretion for exemptions should be on a case-by-case basis.

The March of Dimes testimony illustrates the theme of infant health benefits well, arguing:

> Breast milk provides the ideal amounts of protein, sugar, fat, and most vitamins a baby needs for healthy growth and development. Studies show breast-fed babies are less likely than formula-fed babies to have ear infections, lower respiratory tract infections, meningitis, urinary tract infections, vomiting, and diarrhea. (Danielle Huckins)

The theme of the need for societal support for breastfeeding in order for it to be successful can be illustrated by the testimony of a physician from Children's Mercy Hospital who said, "It is important that we support mothers who have the desire and are dedicated to providing the best nutrition for their children (Kennedy)." Nursing mother Amy Swan also emphasized this point in her 2006 testimony before the Senate committee:

> What happened to me at the health club was one of the most degrading and humiliating experiences of my life. What was always such a natural and beautiful experience for me was now being treated as a very shameful "act" that I should have been doing in private. I still continued to breastfeed my daughter in public, but felt very self-conscious every time I nursed her. Unfortunately, other women who have such an experience may choose to either stop nursing altogether, or opt to take along formula or a bottle because they don't want to offend anyone or be accused of "exposing" themselves. It doesn't seem fair

> that a bottle-fed baby in Kansas has fewer restrictions than my daughter sim-
> ply because my daughter is nourished with mother's milk.

Swan's statement that bottle-fed babies have fewer restrictions because they can eat whenever they want without fear of reprisal is interesting in light of the fact that breastfeeding is the current prevailing medical advice women are receiving from the AAP. It demonstrates the precarious position women are placed in when breastfeeding is highly recommended by the medical commu-nity but bottle feeding often remains the acceptable and expected form of feeding in public. It is clear to see that these messages are in conflict, and that the active lives of today's women and infants are not being recognized and fully welcomed.

Swan's testimony raises some interesting issues about who is being re-stricted in the public space. While many women do in fact choose a combina-tion of breastfeeding and bottle feeding, other women choose to exclusively breastfeed or their children refuse bottles. The focus of the public breastfeed-ing controversy on adult women acting inappropriately in the public space is misdirected. Since this is the way the child eats, an infant is being denied comfort and nourishment in order to accommodate others in the public space that may be uncomfortable. Presumably, adults can look away or move to another location without nearly the amount of distress caused to an infant by interrupting a feeding. Swan's testimony rightly switches the focus to the infant, whose needs should be the focus of concern. However the child hap-pens to eat, an infant needs to be fed wherever he or she may be. The focus instead on adult needs, and whether an infant's mother is considering the feelings of adults in the public space when simply feeding her infant, shows that women and infants are not being fully accepted into the public space.

In other situations, infants with their mothers are practically treated like celebrities, especially when they are very young (and quiet). People rush over to look at the baby and gush about their own children, or may be quick to give up a seat on a bus or lend a hand with luggage. What makes the act of nursing that infant in public so threatening to some? Charkoudian and others (Carter 1995; Stearns 1999) have argued that the act transgresses the boun-daries of the public and private spheres. It brings the private into the public and the public into the private, blurring lines that have kept caregiving in the realm of the private, unseen, unappreciated, under-valued, and misunder-stood.

If one has only the image of the sexual breast as a reference, witnessing a baby at a woman's breast can be disturbing to some people. Swan's experi-ence of the male health club patron concerned about his son witnessing the "act" of breastfeeding is telling. A child has no sexual context for oral-breast contact, so a straightforward answer of "that is how some babies eat" would presumably be readily accepted by a young child. The story also illustrates how infrequently breastfeeding is seen in public in many places in the United States since the parent appears unprepared and panicked to have to explain this behavior.

Also, one is left to wonder if women using a combination of feeding methods are truly choosing freely or if they choose out of fear of offending others or being humiliated when they are out in public with their infants. With 79.2 percent of American women who gave birth in 2011 doing some breastfeeding, one wonders if they might breastfeed longer if the public space were more welcoming (CDC 2014). The idea of providing a genuine choice to women in infant-feeding decisions can also be seen in the letter written to Representative Morrison of the Kansas House of Representatives on February 14, 2005, by lactation consultant Christy Pate:

> As you may know, becoming a parent can be the most overwhelming task a person ever undertakes. Selecting their baby's nutrition is just one of hundreds of decisions many new parents weigh with their baby's best interest at heart. It is so sad that we live in a culture that often pushes parents to decide against breastfeeding a baby. This decision may be the right one for many parents, but is it ever the right one if it is made out of fear of embarrassment, social ostracism, or criminal prosecution?

While Pate is a lactation consultant and clearly an advocate of breastfeeding, her letter recognizes that not all women breastfeed. She recognizes this a decision that can involve both parents, thus separating the issue from child-bearing, as Law (2000) cautions us to do.

Pate's testimony argues that creating societal support for public breast-feeding is the only way to make breastfeeding truly possible for many women. While breastfeeding is a practice that is in need of broad societal support in order for women to have a real choice to do it or not, that does not mean that all women must breastfeed or that an advocacy approach that tries to shame women should be advocated.

The important thing to note is that a position of support for breastfeeding legislation can be taken without naturalizing the role of women as nurturers by recognizing the obvious fact of personal control over one's body. If we fail to give proper notice to the embodied experience of breastfeeding, it can be easy to treat breast vs. bottle as a choice between two types of food rather than one between continuing the biological process of lactation that generally occurs after birth and buying a product to feed the baby. Humans beings can have a diversity of needs at different points in their lives, but recognizing that and enacting policies and practices to support them does not mean they need to be proscribed to certain roles. This thinking gets beyond the equality difference debate and shows that it is a false distinction (Carter 1995). Being restricted for lactating and breastfeeding amounts to exclusion for being a woman; this hurts all women, whether they breastfeed or not. Certainly this is an issue that feminists need to engage with on a political level and not just in academic discussions. To take this position does not mean one thinks everyone must breastfeed, just that every woman that does should have a right to do so without being restricted.

This lack of political engagement in the issue of breastfeeding rights by women's and civil rights groups can be seen in the case of the Kansas pubic breastfeeding law. The groups that testified in the case of HB 2284 represented the medical community, breastfeeding advocacy groups, and nursing mothers and their families. While the law asserts a right to breastfeed, which affects women a great deal, women's rights groups were not involved in testifying or writing letters in this case.

While the local NOW chapter did not testify in the Kansas case (nor did other women's rights groups), the official NOW position supports state breastfeeding rights laws as well as federal legislation to support breastfeeding. Further involvement by NOW chapters that do support legislation in their states could help to better represent the view that all parents' infant-feeding choices need to be supported, especially in light of the fact that 79.2 percent of women who gave birth in 2011 in the United States did some breastfeeding. This could be done without naturalizing the role of women as mothers and nurturers, but by emphasizing the support of women's control over the lactation functions of their bodies and infant-feeding decisions in general.

The responses of breastfeeding activists, ordinary women, and the medical community, to cases of harassment for breastfeeding in public have helped bring the issue of societal support for breastfeeding to the attention of legislators, the public, corporations, and owners of public accommodations. It may be too soon to tell if the nurse-in and other techniques of direct action have an effect on the acceptance of public breastfeeding. Some have argued that the forms of activism described above have had a negative effect on public support for breastfeeding in the public space.

Defining Public Breastfeeding Through Activism

The case of public breastfeeding may demonstrate some limitations to the current approach to protecting breastfeeding through state laws (most of which do not have enforcement provisions), since so many of the stories involved states that already have breastfeeding laws. While no state defines breastfeeding as indecent exposure, how does the public tend to view it? An analysis of articles and comments about public breastfeeding and nurse-ins shows that breastfeeding is frequently compared to sexual activity, as well as urinating or defecating in public. For example, after the incident at the Concord Mall in Delaware, one commenter said that since he could not suck his wife's boob in public, women could not breastfeed in public. While this comment seems extreme and immature, comments of this nature are common from both men and women in response to on-line articles about public breastfeeding or nurse-in stories. Public opinion data also shows that only 43 percent of the United States population thinks public breastfeeding is appropriate (HHS 2011).

In discussing the problematic nature of public breastfeeding, Carter (1995) states, "Women apparently are expected to be actively heterosexual but to avoid drawing attention to sexuality where it is connected to reproduction." Carter's statement shows that the problem is not women being sexualized, which appears to be readily accepted in the culture. She says, "What appears to be disturbing is the very particular form of 'sexuality' which is observed when breast-feeding takes place in public places. Current dominant discourses of active heterosexually . . . expect women's bodies to be sexualized—but in ways which signal heterosexual availability and involvement" (Carter 1995, 119)." This explains the accounts of aversion to breastfeeding by some employees from the above mentioned stores despite walls adorned with pictures of women in bras and underwear or young teenagers embracing boys while wearing bikinis.

A commenter to the November 18, 2010 post by Michele, "Conclusion: Breastfeeding Is Sexual and Totally Disgusting" on the Daily Momtra site articulated the same ideas as Carter (1995) in everyday language. In trying to explain her take on the negative reaction of many people to public breast-feeding, Misty wrote:

> Here is why I [sic] think people have such a problem with it and not with other cleavage-baring things . . . it is simply because it bothers them to see something that THEY consider sexual in an non-sexual situation . . . with a baby involved. so, I [sic] think it bothers them that they are like "whoa, boobs!" But they can't really enjoy it because of the baby . . . if that makes sense. But [sic] if you were showing the same amount of flesh with a revealing shirt or dress, they'd love it because they would feel free to ogle.

Both men and women have expressed concerns that breastfeeding appears sexual or that it is comparable to urinating or defecating in public. For example, one woman responded to a June 12, 2014, post entitled, "Breastfeeding and More" on the site *Motherhood and More* wrote:

> I hate to sat [sic] it, but I pretty much disagree on every point you have made. I have 4 kids, have breastfed, and totally think it is wrong to do it in public, without covering up. There are those (women), who think it is gross, looks sexual, and who worry about what other people see and how they may make others feel uncomfortable.

The following comment posted in response to a *Washington Post* article by
Janice D'Arcy on May 10, 2012, entitled, *"Time* Cover Issues a Challenge to
Those Who Support Nursing" is also typical of many I read:

> It seems to me that people who do this publicly do it for the shock value and
> because they really don't care if people around them are uncomfortable. Bodi-
> ly functions are completely natural also. Is the next step just foregoing a
> restroom and "doing" it wherever you are?

While anonymous comments do not necessarily represent the thoughts of
most people, they do show the parameters of the debate and which arguments
frequently get raised. The common themes were public sex, urinating or
defecating in public, and the idea that women are seeking attention when
they breastfeed in a public place. No state I know of treats breastfeeding in
public as indecent exposure akin to urinating or having sex in public, yet
people made this association in almost every set of comments I have reviewed in over ten years of reading public breastfeeding stories online. Why
is this the case? Breastfeeding so frequently continues to be kept out of view
in the United States. The association is made because so many men and
women are much more familiar with breasts in a sexual context. In particular,
oral-breast contact is seen in a sexual light, because for many adults, this is
the only context with which they are familiar. Many people have never seen
anyone breastfeeding. We do not associate eating in other contexts as akin to
sexual activity or eliminating bodily waste, nor should we in the case of
breastfeeding. Unfortunately, it will take seeing breastfeeding in public for it
to be accepted, but the stigma could keep some women who want to breastfeed from doing so.

Some could argue that keeping breastfeeding out of sight is appropriate
given that breastfeeding is a bodily function involving parts that are normally
covered with clothing in public. I would argue, however, that eating in general is a bodily function, and that some people only associate breastfeeding
more with urination and sex than with eating because it is so rare to see this
form of eating in public. Breasts are not genitalia, yet they repeatedly get
compared to the primary sex organs. This fact makes it uncomfortable for
people to see women's breasts in babies' mouths. A common comment on
the part of harassed women was that the baby or a cover was blocking sight
of the areola and all or most of the breast; thus, it seems that the activity itself
is what is often disturbing to people rather than just the sight of the breast.

Keeping women and their breast-feeding children out of the public sphere
is clearly discriminatory. It is difficult for many to see it that way because we
have kept what is not indecent or sexual out of the public sphere for so long
that it makes many people very uncomfortable. Some have never seen it and
their children have never seen it. The nurse-in participants are doing more

than protesting a company or employee; they are taking back the public space and opening it up to all women and their children. Many comments refer to breastfeeding women as "shoving their breasts in people's faces"; yet with the few experiences I have had where someone was breastfeeding in public, the opposite was the case. Similar to the Stearns (1999) study, in my own interviews with women I found the goal of breastfeeding mothers was to be as discreet as possible. Given Carter's analysis, the "attention-seeking" and "in your face" comments are not surprising. They reveal an expectation that mothering still occurs in a private place (Carter 1995).

Charkoudian argues that nursing in front of others also opened people up in the most unexpected ways. She relates a story of what happened when she nursed in front of her grandfather and how he started to talk to her about things they had never discussed before. She related this in the interview:

> "My grandfather used to ask me to hide it, but once he accepted it, he told me this amazing story about how he was nursed until he was five, because it was in the middle of the Armenian genocide and his mother had to nurse all four of her kids because they needed it for sustenance. So that was a really amazing transformation to see." (Regales 2005)

Charkoudian gets at something here that goes beyond just individual rights to choose to breastfeed. Her story about her grandfather allows us to envision the effects that bringing mothering into the public space will have and how it can transform one's perspective on what is important. Indeed, one of the most disturbing things about critical comments about public breastfeeding stories is how the child and his or her needs become almost invisible.

In many countries, no one gives a second thought to women with their infants in slings nursing when the need arises. This is true, even in societies that have more conservative norms of behavior than the United States (Van Esterik 1989; Kedrowski and Lipscomb 2008). For example my obstetrician, who was from Ghana, once said to me, "People breastfeed everywhere in Ghana." At the same time, norms pertaining to appropriate dress as well as views about sexual morality in Ghana are much more conservative than in the United States.

Not all women breastfeed, but opening the public space to both women who breastfeed and women who use bottles is not only reasonable, but is necessary in a free and democratic society. Otherwise, we never really opened up the public space to women; it was only opened up to women who can pass as men, which obviously breastfeeding women cannot do. Around the turn of the twentieth century when breastfeeding was still the norm, women were not in the public space to the degree they are now. In a non-mothering context, women's inclusion into society has been largely regarded as positive. Over 80 percent of adults in the United States say that men and women should have equal roles in society (Norrander 2008). Today, more women want to be in public space and to breastfeed their children. Why shouldn't they? Shouldn't infants whose mothers' have decided to breastfeed be free to eat when and where they please just as babies who drink from bottles?

These ideas have been expressed by many of the breastfeeding mothers, whose stories have generated activism, but the arguments are not always framed explicitly as civil rights or women's rights issues. This may present a challenge to sustained activism if there is no broader movement to which it is connected. Being part of a broader social movement gives activists an alternative community of like-minded individuals that could prevent them from getting disillusioned and giving up hope as the broader society continues to attempt to shame and silence them (Woliver 1993).

I interviewed an attorney and breastfeeding advocate who said:

> The direction to go in for me is a civil rights frame. It's that this is public space and it belongs to me as much as it belongs to you, and so the norms of behavior in public spaces are as much determined by my needs as yours are. . . . So public space is everybody's and everybody gets to determine what the rules are; everybody has to be accepted in it and if you don't like it, you have to go home. It's a rejection of hegemony.

This statement relates well to the nurse-in women's stories. They are asserting a right to the public space regardless of the fact that they are lactating.

The idea here is for the offended person to leave the space or look away rather than for the woman feeding a hungry child at the breast to leave the space. A frequent quip heard in other situations is, "If you don't like it, don't look." Yet when I raise the issue of public breastfeeding, even with liberal colleagues, I typically hear about how uncomfortable it makes people feel, rather than this old adage.

Some might see this argument as one of anything goes. A closer analysis shows that "being who you are" doesn't mean doing anything you want in public but that the rules for public space need to protect the minority as well as the majority. The advocate quoted above went on to say this:

> I've always couched it in civil rights terms. We have viewed equal rights as the right to be a white man but real civil rights is the right to be whoever you are. To be safe, to have kids, to not have kids, be in public space, don't be in public space. The public space belongs to everybody whether you are the majority or the minority. And if you rack up the numbers, white men are not the majority anymore so why are they still controlling the mores of public space?

One might argue (as many have in online discussions) that while breastfeeding is important and is to be encouraged, asking women to use a private space is not unreasonable. Since many young infants often nurse every two hours, an infant could get hungry right after his or her mother enters a store or while waiting in an older child's pediatrician's waiting room. Packing up a wailing infant, the stroller, and the other children to go find a private place to nurse seems far more imposing to the woman who simply seeks to feed her child, than simply having any offended parties look away or move. The other problem with this approach is that it continues to keep nursing in the closet so that it is not modeled as a common and culturally acceptable method to feed an infant. Rather it leaves us in a place where women are asked to "do their duty in private" (Carter 1995).

A civil rights approach, on the other hand, focuses more on inclusion and on the needs of the individual to be accepted as one is—male or female, lactating or not. The idea of civil rights as the right to be a white man means essentially that in order to use the public space, one has to *pass as a man* by not having any needs that he would not have, such as the need to nurse a child. It uses men as the default human being instead of truly recognizing human diversity. It is important to point out that due to the physiology of nursing, the need to nurse becomes mutual as a breast that is not regularly relieved of milk can cause problems such as leaking, cogged ducts, and mastasis (an infection that can leave women quite sick). Thus, having to appear to be non-lactating in public can create quite a hardship for both woman and child.

Casual suggestions to solve the problem by feeding pumped milk with a bottle whenever one is in public ignore some of the basic facts about supply and demand with breastfeeding. But, more importantly, they fail to interrogate the reasons underlying the lack of comfort with public breastfeeding and accept a severe limitation on women simply because they are lactating. Annie Reneau (2014) gave this response to similar suggestions from those uncomfortable with breastfeeding in public on her blog, *Motherhood and More*, on July 10, 2014:

> But the real answer to this question is they shouldn't have to. Think about what you're suggesting: that a mother skip a feeding to pump, or pump regularly enough to have the extra milk to pump outside of a feeding, then find a way to keep the milk cold in transport, then find a way to warm up the milk once she is where she's going, then feed the baby with the bottled milk, then deal with the leakage or discomfort of the full breasts she has from feeding with the bottle instead of the breast for that feeding, and then wash and sterilize the bottle afterward—all instead of just taking her baby with her and feeding the ready-to-go milk she has on hand in her own body?

The idea of the right to breastfeed in public as a feminist issue has been expressed in many places in the online advocacy community as well. The following post from August 26, 2012, by a blogger known as Blue Milk posting on the blog site *Feministe*, entitled, "Why Breastfeeding is a Feminist Issue," captures this line of thinking well:

> Breastfeeding is a feminist issue not because mummy bloggers like me say
> it is, but because it's about working to ensure that women and their bodies are
> considered as important (as normal) as men and their bodies. Something happens for all of us—regardless of whether we are breastfeeders or not—when a
> woman is allowed to breastfeed, in public, as a member of her community,
> while getting shit done in her life—it makes a statement that women belong,
> that women's bodies belong, that women are here.

In response to feminist critics of breastfeeding advocacy, she goes on to say this:

> When feminists write about these tensions for mothers there is a tendency to
> argue that because it is so difficult to breastfeed in these circumstances that we
> need to back off about breastfeeding. I'm a little skeptical of this strategy,
> though I think it comes from a good place. Women are entitled to their
> choices, of course . . . but isn't it awfully convenient that we never question the
> institutions of power that happen to arrange themselves in such a way that
> women have little real choice about breastfeeding?

Some have argued that more public nursing could make non-breastfeeding mothers feel bad, yet the issue does not have to be approached in this way. If women are truly to have free choice about infant feeding, both bottle and breastfeeding need to be perfectly acceptable in the public space. It is not breastfeeding in public itself that makes women who do not breastfeed feel bad, but an approach that focuses primarily on their behavior or "lifestyle choice" instead of addressing the problems of an unsupportive environment and inadequate family leave.

The two types of feeding need to coexist. Indeed, for the most part they do. Many parents I talked to who used either feeding method or a combination of both said they did what they felt was best for their families, and that they make no judgment of others' decisions. For example, Erin D. who had used formula to feed all six of her children, after switching from breastfeeding with her first child in the early weeks said, "I didn't know anyone who formula fed. I didn't get anything from them. No problems. I would like to think that most people just don't care. I don't know, I just feel like they shouldn't care. I am a good mother and I didn't breastfeed." On the other hand, a woman I interviewed who breastfed all four of her children for one to two years said, "I believe children should be breastfed if at all possible, but if I see a woman using a bottle, I don't judge. I assume there is a reason." However, the fact that public breastfeeding cases do make headlines and that they produce a lot of very emotional feedback shows that we still have a long way to go to achieve a public space open to all.

Another common theme I saw in the comment threads after articles about nurse-ins was the idea that having a child and choosing to breastfeed is a private or personal choice. In other words, one should not have a child unless they are willing and able to bear all of the costs on their own, such as breastfeeding in private, leaving a job to nurse children, and not making demands for pumping rooms, nursing rooms, or onsite child care. These comments are in the vein of the child-free movement whose characterization of childbearing and childrearing as a private decision akin to the decision to purchase a boat or a car has been critiqued by Erin Taylor (2003). This perspective does not take into account that democracy depends on care work that is done in the supposedly private realm, mostly by women (Kittay 1999; Woliver 2002; Tronto 2013).

In the case of pregnancy, Congress clearly rejected this idea by passing the Pregnancy Discrimination Act of 1979. Extending this idea to breastfeeding at the federal level as Carolyn Maloney has proposed could be one step in the right direction (Kedrowski and Lipscomb 2008). Judith Galtry (2000) has also written about this approach. The accounts in this chapter show, however, that legislation alone is not enough. This is demonstrated by the number of media stories of public breastfeeding harassment that are happening in states with public breastfeeding laws (Ford 2013; Leckie 2010; Regales 2005; Rochman 2011). Breastfeeding advocate Jacqueline Wolf (2008) specifically addresses the issue of cultural acceptance as a key element to women's ability to breastfeed successfully.

Wolf (2008) attributes the low exclusivity rates and duration rates of breastfeeding in the United States with a culture that is not supportive of public breastfeeding. She recognizes the paradox of the United States being a bottle-feeding culture while at the same time strongly encouraging breastfeeding. She argues that the sexualization of the breast in the United States is one of the major reasons for the discomfort with public breastfeeding. Wolf (2008) explains, "Americans think breasts are primarily for enhancing sexual activity, which results in widespread discomfort when they are reminded that breasts go into babies' mouths." She illustrates the cultural variability of these attitudes by relating an exchange one of her graduate students had with a Samoan woman while she was there engaging in field work. The woman was amazed to learn that adult American men frequently suck on women's breasts as part of sexual activity. In response to this information, she reportedly asked if American men enjoyed pretending that they were infants. Wolf (2008) goes on to point out that public breastfeeding in many countries is "as mundane as public conversation."

She explains that for those who "work on breastfeeding," the public breastfeeding problem is too quickly dismissed or not seen as a major problem or barrier to breastfeeding. She argues, that in fact, this is a major reason why exclusive breastfeeding rates are so low. She states, "The negative attitude toward public breastfeeding is a cornerstone of low breastfeeding rates and a basis of our persistently formula feeding culture" (Wolf 2008). While Wolf does not argue that Americans should try to imitate Samoans, she does argue that there are consequences to the American breast obsession. She says, "Women who have successfully breastfed for long periods of time know that unless women can feed their babies anytime, anywhere, they're going to end up housebound." She goes on to say that since many women will find this exclusion and isolation intolerable, they switch to using bottles, which is demonstrated by the dramatic drop in exclusive breastfeeding rates even at six weeks when over half of babies were receiving some formula.

Wolf is right to bring attention to the cultural acceptance of public breast-feeding that is often not the focus of breastfeeding advocates. This is because even with parental leave policies, implementation of workplace lactation programs, and on-site day care, these things all do nothing to change the culture that is hostile to public breastfeeding, particularly in some regions of the United States. Wolf aptly describes how breastfeeding is deemed a good thing, but then uninformed suggestions are made that imply that there should be no need for breastfeeding in public with a little advanced planning. She points out how human milk is designed for infants to nurse frequently, which is why so many women in other cultures wear their babies for easy access to nursing (Wolf 2008). Again, however, to support a woman who decides to nurse on demand wherever she is does not mean one has to shame those who have chosen differently. It is crucial that we separate the issue of appropriate approaches to breastfeeding advocacy from the discussion of the right to breastfeed in public. One can envision people who support the latter holding a wide variety of opinions on the former.

Backlash? Do Nurse-Ins Hurt the Cause?

Stearns' (1999) found that the women she interviewed had not been harassed for breastfeeding in public. Her research reveals that many women who do breastfeeding in public conceal it as much as humanly possible. By being discreet, they can feed their children as they wish, but they also accept the culture of sexualization of the breast by being sure to keep the breast hidden. As Stearns explains, "In describing how they breastfeed, women uniformly emphasized the importance and or necessity of learning to breastfeed dis-creetly" (312). She goes on to say, "Being an invisible breastfeeding mother was the goal for many women." (313). Stearns's work shows the need to open up the public space fully to all women, lactating or not.

Some argue that the spontaneous activism that has developed online actu-ally hurts the cause of women who wish to breastfeed in public and may scare away mothers from breastfeeding. Clarke (2014) argues that the use of the direct action approach of nurse-ins actually hurts the cause of nursing mothers because it calls attention to horror stories and makes a "big deal" out of nursing. She argues that simply nursing in public is the best approach to making it a more common practice. According to Clarke, this will reduce any problems and lead to other women feeling comfortable enough to breastfeed as well.

In analyzing articles posted about women who are harassed for breast-feeding in public, many comments are supportive, but they are always accompanied by negative comments from both men and women. A common theme is to equate public breastfeeding with sex acts and defecation and urination. This issue was discussed earlier in the chapter when exploring the way public breastfeeding is defined, but it also comes up in discussions about whether the nurse-ins actually throw fuel on the fire and encourage attitudes that challenge public breastfeeding. Here is one example that followed an article about a woman who was refused access to a Victoria's Secret dressing room to nurse her baby after spending over one hundred dollars on merchandise when the store was mostly empty. The commenter says, "I am female and I do not approve of breastfeeding wherever you take a notion. You moms say oh this is natural . . . will [sic] so is peeing and pooping and having sex but I don't want you doing that in the restaurant seat beside me. Are you Moms too lazy you cannot get to a more appropriate place like the privacy of your car when you are out? I think you just like showing your breasts."

Some comments that are supportive of breastfeeding, still argue against the attention given in the media to this issue. The comment below was posted in response to an article appearing in the *Huffiington Post*, written by Mandy Velez on January 16, 2014:

> Can't help but notice the absurd amount of media attention that revolves around breastfeeding mothers being judged. There are very few other topics where one person's ignorance in a private setting is blown out of proportion to this degree. For the record, I breastfeed my son, but I've noticed WAY more judgment toward mothers who feed their child formula. Not to mention, other [breastfeeding] moms are usually the ones doing the judging. On the contrary, it's generally ignorant non-parents judging the breastfeeding moms. Believe me, some cases piss me off. But a sales clerk at an underwear store? C'mon people. There's no reason to make a perceived problem like this worse. Or at least talk to the person directly instead of writing a blog, and blaming the whole company.

While not all breastfeeding advocates and nursing moms see the direct action approach as appropriate or productive, this may be because they do not wish to really challenge the social order. Others worry that these approaches send a message that is unsupportive of those who do not breastfeed; a different sort of activism online has begun in this vein. The above comment shows yet again, that the issue of the right to breastfeed in public is being conflated with the issue of breastfeeding advocacy. Until these two issues are separated and addressed head-on, the current paradox of women being urged to breastfeed for at least a year with very little cultural support will continue.

Not Everybody Breastfeeds: Activism Supporting Bottle Feeding

With LLL, the AAP, and the medical/public health community advocating breastfeeding and feminists not coming to the forefront of infant feeding policy, where do those who bottle feed (formula or breast milk) find support? As Susanne Barston (2012) points out in her book, *Bottled Up: How Breastfeeding Has Come to Define Motherhood and Why It Shouldn't*, many women experience little support for bottle feeding. After her own experiences of trying to breastfeed her son while suffering from post-partum depression and many other challenges, Barston started a blog to support those who use bottles. The blog is called the *Fearless Formula Feeder* (FFF) and is found at http://www.fearlessformulafeeder.com.

The FFF blog was also featured along with a few others on a website called *Bottle Babies* started by a woman in Australia who had difficulties breastfeeding and switched to formula feeding. The site is described as a supportive place for anyone who is bottle feeding in part or full, pumped milk or formula. It asserts that infant feeding is a parent's choice and that women need to support each other's decisions. The site points out the vast array of support groups for breastfeeding and the lack of support for bottle-feeding parents. This is ironic because in Australia, 82 percent of babies at six months are not exclusively fed breast milk. This means the vast majority of infants there are consuming some formula, which is similar to the situation in the United States.

The *Bottle-Babies* non-profit organization was founded in Australia and can now be found on Facebook. *Bottle Babies* has partnered with FFF on a video entitled, "I am a bottle baby and I . . ." The video shows healthy, joyful, contented, bonded, intelligent children who are loved and adored by their parents. The entries and comments on the FFF blog and those associated with the *Bottle Babies* site demonstrate just how deep this issue runs. Most parents deeply love and care for their children, so statistics about formula leading to increased disease, less attachment, and even lowered intelligence can be deeply painful to those who use formula, especially if they wanted to breastfeed but experienced endless problems after intense efforts.

The above sites provide support for parents using bottles, while also asserting that they are decidedly not anti-breastfeeding. They seek support online from others with shared experiences and oppose the shaming they have sometimes experienced for not breastfeeding. The existence of these sites speaks to the need to eliminate shaming from the advocacy of breastfeeding, as has been discussed in chapter 4 and advocated by Hausman

(2012), Taylor and Wallace (2012), and others. This approach might be more effective in building a broader coalition of women supporting breastfeeding through social inclusion and public policy.

An Activism that Balances Rights with Public Responsibilities

This chapter has documented the varied ways that activism on the part of mothers has brought attention to the issue of breastfeeding rights. While public breastfeeding laws and corporate practices are important, many of these direct-action efforts have been more episodic and reactive rather than on-going efforts to transform the overall social environment to better support breastfeeding.

The grassroots political activities studied in this chapter all focused on breastfeeding rights. While a civil rights approach is important because it defines who is included in the community, this approach alone will not help give every woman who desires to breastfeed the opportunity to do so. Since society depends on mothers and all parents in the work they do raising children, then it is reasonable to expect policy to go beyond simply allowing women to breastfeed in public (a negative right), but to provide positive support of this endeavor. Mary Ann Glendon, for example, has critiqued the focus solely on rights in American law, arguing, "We should not have to apologize for defining our society as one that relies heavily on families to socialize our young citizens and that encourages, aids, and rewards persons who perform family obligations" (Glendon 1991, 135).

By not discussing public responsibilities to support those nurturing children, women shoulder much of the burden. This is not to say that rights are not important, but they need to be balanced with the idea that society also has a responsibility to support the work done to nurture our "young citizens." There have been some coalitions formed between the breastfeeding advocacy community and other groups, such as Moms Rising, but there is not a great deal of ongoing activism around family policy issues.

Paid family leave at the state level is one possible avenue for channeling activism supportive of breastfeeding in a way that can help women address the financial issues that may make sustained breastfeeding challenging for some women. An article on *The Huffington Post* on July 2, 2014, by Maria Shriver, discusses California's tenth anniversary of its paid family-leave program and its effects on breastfeeding, employment, and family income. Shriver wrote:

> Since the law's passage, research has confirmed that paid family leave offers real and lasting benefits both to families and to employers. Mothers and fathers are getting increased bonding time with newborns. Breastfeeding rates have almost doubled for mothers who take leave. There are lower rates of postpartum depression, and health outcomes among children have improved . . . In

fact, an overwhelming majority of employers report that providing family leave has a neutral or even positive impact on productivity and their bottom line.

As an activist, Shriver is attempting to spread the word to other activists that this type of policy is possible at the state level. She specifically mentions the positive effects the policy has had for breastfeeding, which should catch the attention of those specifically focused on this issue, and also mentions the other positive effects for families. A report on the first ten years of the law shows that many women used the program in order to spend an additional six weeks with their infants, while they would have otherwise only had six weeks total. While some women (outside the three states with paid leave) currently take twelve weeks maternity leave under the federal Family and Medical Leave Act of 1993, many are unable to do so because the leave is unpaid.

Activism for paid family leave is one approach to helping parents spend more time with their infants, which can also help women reach their breastfeeding goals. Focusing on paid family leave such as those policies currently operating in California, New Jersey, and Rhode Island can also help with the distribution of labor problem, in which married and cohabitating women are doing a disproportionate share of the child-care work. For example, in the first ten years of the paid family-leave program, California experienced a dramatic increase in the percentage of men taking paid family leave. This can also help women with breastfeeding goals because spouses can get paid time off to assist with the other child-care duties, freeing up women who wish to breastfeed.

This chapter has explored a wide range of activities in support of breastfeeding and some in support for bottle-feeding mothers. The activity that has received the most attention in the media is the grassroots organized nurse-in, used in response to a breastfeeding mother's harassment in a public setting. These activities seek to bring attention to the issue of public breastfeeding and state laws that protect the practice.

I found that the online discussions surrounding these events take on another dimension. The events spark a conversation online about what public breastfeeding is and how it is best categorized. In response to nurse-in activities critical online comments consistently compare the behavior to having sex or going to the bathroom. Online critics of public breastfeeding completely ignore the issue of dependency and best interests of the infant to eat in the way he or she is usually fed, and focus completely on how the child's mother makes others feel in the public space or on how her behavior is attention-seeking. Supporters of public breastfeeding consistently argue that breastfeeding is eating and should be no more offensive than bottle feeding in public.

The sporadic nature of the nurse-ins and the fact that harassment seems to continue in states with public breastfeeding laws demonstrates that the activities may have a limited effect in normalizing public breastfeeding. They are not consistently being carried out in the same locations over a period of time as were the lunch counter sit-ins (Laue 1989). In and of themselves they don't really apply enough pressure for business practice to change. Charkodian attempted to change corporate policy at Starbucks through a letter-writing campaign in addition to the nurse-in. The subsequent media attention and conversations online about the meaning of public breastfeeding may have an effect in engaging a broader section of the public on the subject, as she was interviewed about the activism as many as two years later.

The fact that harassment for public breastfeeding continued to occur in states that already had public breastfeeding laws shows that the nurse-in approach may be limited. Rather than organizing nurse-ins to either show the need for a state law or get people to follow one that already exists, working to get laws that are enforceable is a more effective approach to changing the behavior of owners' of public accommodations. Marcus (2011) explains that while most state breastfeeding laws do not have an enforcement provision, ten states do have them. She argues that working to get these provisions added to laws that do not have them is a strong strategy for advocates to take to protect breastfeeding in public.

In her article, "Lactation in the Law Revisited" (first printed in *Mothering* and available on her website http://www.breastfeedinglaw.com), Marcus tells the story of Anna (not her real name) who was harassed for breastfeeding in the toddler area of a pool in the state of Washington in 2010. Anna has some means of recourse because in 2009, the state amended its civil rights law pertaining to public accommodations to prohibit discrimination against women who are breastfeeding. She filed a complaint with the Washington Civil Rights Commission. The action is ongoing. Marcus points out that Anna has concealed her identity since she did not want mothers to organize a nurse-in; rather, she wanted the pool owners to be held accountable for their actions.

Some fear the nurse-in approach can cause a backlash and scare mothers away from breastfeeding in public by publicizing a few horror stories. Critics point out that most women who nurse in public report no problems. While LLL members are sometimes involved in these kinds of activities, I have found that many leaders of breastfeeding support organizations take an approach of simply nursing whenever and wherever their babies are hungry and encouraging others to do the same. In this way, the act becomes normalized simply because people are doing it. Some also spoke of approaching nursing mothers and thanking them to show solidarity, as LLL leader and IBCLC Julie Clark explained in chapter 3.

Clark's approach to activism is to engage in breastfeeding and show support to others who are breastfeeding. Simply increasing the numbers of women nursing in public could have more of an effect than laws specifying it as a right given the number of stories covered here that occur in states where a public breastfeeding law already exists (Ford 2013; Leckie 2010; Regales 2005; Rochman 2011). Erin F. was training as a La Leche Leader when she spoke to me about her goal of directly supporting breastfeeding mothers and of raising more peaceful children. Russell Dalton calls this engaged citizenship because it seems to reject formal politics but, instead, seeks to make different individual choices, such as not buying formula and rejecting consumerism (Dalton 2008). This also goes along with the blog comments above that one way to change the culture is to be willing to act in ways that may be controversial or unpopular. While engaged citizenship can help change the culture to a degree, it does not address the substantive issues that can serve as constraints to breastfeeding, such as needing to return to work and not having access to one's children or pumping facilities at work.

Coalitions for Action on Policy Related to Breastfeeding

Much of the policy activism related to breastfeeding has been focused on public breastfeeding laws, which can be an important step in making sure that the community is inclusive and that women and their children are not kept out of the public space due to breastfeeding. On the other hand, creating an environment in which the care work of both men and women is valued will take more than inclusion alone. Both public and private business policies that support parenting more generally will also help provide the opportunity for women to breastfeed if they wish. Some companies have had great success with on-site day care, which they have found to be profitable and not just convenient for their employees. Workers were, according to some studies, more productive and missed less time due to child-care related issues (Connelly, DeGraf and Wills 2004). While this type of program can help parents regardless of feeding method, being able to nurse children on the premises during breaks is a benefit for those who are breastfeeding.

Building coalitions with others beyond those involved directly in breastfeeding advocacy can go a long way in producing the kind of change in policy that would help make breastfeeding possible for more women. The United States Breastfeeding Committee (which has over fifty member organizations including Moms Rising) provides toolkits and information about lobbying on its website at USbreastfeeding.org. MomsRising.org has family leave listed first on its "Our Issues" page of the website, and includes testimony from families and model legislation for which members can lobby.

In the area of state-paid family leave, there is some room to building on the experiences of California, New Jersey, and Rhode Island. Working toward a national paid leave policy such as the FAMILY Act supported by Moms Rising and NOW is another option. Coalitions between NOW, Moms

Rising, labor, and breastfeeding advocates could go a long way in making it easier for working mothers to breastfeed, as well as supporting care work more generally. While workplace pumping policies are important, paid leave would provide an additional support for those who wish to use it whether they are breastfeeding or not. Because the program serves a broader range of family needs, coalitions can be formed across a wider range of individuals and may be easier to sustain.

While broader ideological differences may exist between members of such a coalition, common ground on the paid family-leave issue and other policies supportive of breastfeeding and parenting, in general, can be successful in the same way that coalitions of death penalty opponents have joined together from the left and right to abolish the death penalty in some states. For example, in Maryland, the umbrella group CASE Maryland (Maryland Citizens Against the Death Penalty) included groups from across the political spectrum all working together for a common goal. The coalition included many Catholic and other religious organizations, along with groups typically associated with the left, such as the ACLU, the Campaign to End the Death Penalty, Amnesty International, Jonah House, and the War Resisters League. A full list can be found at: www.mdcase.org/node/12.

One potential challenge in building political coalitions to organize and lobby for policies supportive of breastfeeding is that breastfeeding advocates who share a passion for helping women breastfeed on a one-on-one level may well disagree on many political issues. By avoiding political approaches, these differences do not become an issue. Ward (2000) writes about how LLL made a decision not to take a stance on the abortion issue, for example, though some founders wished to do so. One pro-choice breastfeeding advocate told me that many breastfeeding advocates are pro-life, while some are pro-choice. A common commitment to promote breastfeeding links them together.

While women's organization's like NOW may not agree with all of the approaches to breastfeeding advocacy taken by members of USBC, for example, there is agreement on paid family leave, public breastfeeding laws, and protecting workplace pumping. Coalitions can be formed on these issues that the groups hold in common. Involvement of feminist groups on the issue of breastfeeding advocacy, as well, can allow a dialogue so that concerns can be heard.

In the CASE example in Maryland, there is no doubt many supporters were on opposite sides of other political debates, including the abortion debate. Yet they were able to work together to end the death penalty in Maryland in 2013. This is a model that breastfeeding advocates and others seeking policies in support of care work can pursue to help achieve lasting success.

NOTES

1. Appendices are located at the end of the manuscript just before the reference page.

Conclusion

While breastfeeding initiation rates in the United States have greatly increased since the early 1970s, breastfeeding is something of a paradox in this country. On one hand, breastfeeding is highly recommended and promoted as a public health concern, yet public policy, cultural practices, and medical support is still lacking for many women. This causes a majority of them not to meet their own breastfeeding goals. On the other hand, many women using formula for a variety of reasons often feel unsupported because all of the attention seems to be on breastfeeding.

At the same time, a related second paradox exists in which the lines between breast and bottle are blurred, despite the seeming gulf between these two camps. Many babies considered exclusively breastfed drink pumped milk in a bottle, and the majority of babies receive some formula in their first year. Even medical professionals, including lactation consultants, use formula to supplement infants when there is a medical necessity. Thus, both breastfeeding advocates and critics of advocacy share more common ground than is typically thought.

In this book, I explored the existence of these paradoxes in order to discover a better way of supporting women in their infant feeding decisions. While protecting public breastfeeding as a civil rights issue with enforceable laws can create a more inclusive environment for all women and their children, framing the issue as a *negative right* is not enough. While women should not be excluded from public spaces for breastfeeding their children, public policy that goes further by valuing and investing in the caring work parents do is also necessary. Feminist organizations and women's groups like NOW, Moms Rising, and the Third Wave Foundation currently do support breastfeeding rights as well as substantive policy supports, while also condemning the shaming of women who do not breastfeed. This is the correct position for women's groups to take, but more activism across groups is needed. Breastfeeding rights involve the ability to make decisions about the use of one's own body, which feminists have long supported.

However, many breastfeeding advocates and mothers do not always identify with feminism (Tucker 2008; Nathanson 2008). It is important that women come together to support the right to breastfeed, which should be less controversial than abortion rights. While differences on other reproductive and women's issues may present a challenge to building coalitions among women, a failure to do so leaves women unsupported and exacerbates their inequality, regardless of how they feed their infants. I have suggested in chapter 6 that an approach similar to that taken on the death penalty issue can achieve great success by linking groups such as feminists, labor, and mothers' organizations.

The feedback provided by the interviews in chapter 3 also support the idea of activism that focuses on the broader culture and opposes a *politics of shame* championed by some in the public health field, as explored in chapter 5. The women I interviewed for chapter 3 did not tend to speak in terms of feminism, but their views could be called feminist as they were fully supportive of women's inclusion in public and work life. I was encouraged to find the mothers took a non-judgmental stance toward one another.

This is similar to what Tucker (2008) has found, and is also similar to some of the mother activists organizing nurse-ins, as explored in chapter 6. Feminists should work together with other activists to create a more open public space and workplace for lactating women, even if the movements are not explicitly labeled as feminist, in order to broaden their appeal and secure real change that will improve the lives of women and offer them more opportunity to breastfeed (Powell 2008).

An additional area that women's activism must focus on is improvement in medical support for breastfeeding. In chapter 4, I found medical variables, such as hospital practices and lactation consultants to be the most important when it comes to state breastfeeding rates. While the number of lactation consultants is positively related to higher six-month breastfeeding rates, those facing primarily lactation failure (caused by failure of the breast to make milk as opposed to failure of the infant to adequately take milk) may not be receiving adequate diagnosis and often struggle to breastfeed before it is recognized. Further development of medical specialty in this area is needed. Women's Health Centers can be instrumental here by bringing together those with backgrounds in women's studies and public health, as seen in the excellent work of the Breastfeeding and Feminism International Conference health each year in Chapel Hill, North Carolina.

Figures appearing in a June 4, 2012, article by Bonnie Rochman, posted on *Time* online, show that 85 percent of women report that they intend to breastfeed for at least three months, but only 34.2 percent achieve this goal.

Another survey found 60 percent of women fail to meet their own breastfeeding goals. Rather than simply assuming they were unrealistic goals or engaging in useless *mommy wars* about whether women tried hard enough, we can work to make breastfeeding possible for those who do have a goal in mind. Far from essentializing women, this approach values the care work upon which we all depend.

In response to the possible criticism that these policies must somehow inevitably lead to even more pressure to breastfeed and condemnation of those who cannot or do not breastfeed, I have argued that this perception keeps breastfeeding advocates and others with similar views on supportive family policies from joining forces to support societal programs. Without supportive policy and a supportive culture, there is effectively no real choice to breastfeed given economic and social realities. I do recognize that government policy alone cannot accomplish the goal of supporting all women in their infant feeding goals. I propose an approach that sees an expanded role for governmental and non-governmental policy to support parenting more broadly. Policies not directly related to breastfeeding should be gender neutral. Family leave then is better than maternity leave because the latter makes it more difficult for men to be involved in care work. A more equal distribution of care work plays an important role in making breastfeeding a more realistic possibility for many women by freeing up co-parents for other care work tasks.

Failing to invest in care work generally as well as the care work that only women can do (i.e., breastfeeding) is what creates the pressure-filled, stressful environment for some women that puts all the burden on the individual mother. We need to get away from the idea that it is biology itself that oppresses women, and recognize that needs vary across groups in the population and that the public and work space must accommodate these needs. While professional support and hospital practices have improved, the anti-public breastfeeding culture and public policy still have a long way to go. Hopefully, the variables that have been linked to higher and longer nursing rates, such as hospital practices and lactation consultant availability, will lead to more women having the courage to nurse in public. This will change the culture over time as people grow up witnessing breastfeeding across the United States.

It is important to recognize that breastfeeding is not the only way that infants are fed in this country, and that this is unlikely to change. For some women, who very much desired to breastfeed but experienced primary insufficient lactation, increased medical specialization is also needed. There is some evidence that a specialty in this area is beginning to grow; this will be tremendously important as it is estimated that primary lactation failure can affect up to 5 percent of women (Neifert 2001, 278). Finally, more attention is being brought to this problem. Continued women's activism can help shift the existing public health paradigm tended to focus on education of women to one that seeks to change societal conditions in a way that is more conducive to breastfeeding.

Unfortunately, a welcoming public space and more medical expertise on breastfeeding will not alter the challenges that women face when they must or choose to return to work. While law requires some employers to accommodate pumping, the current policy is inadequate. While a more comprehensive policy on pumping is needed that includes all employers, additional solutions are needed such as on-site day care and paid family leaves. Pumping adds a lot of extra work on top of what, for many women, is already a *second shift* (Hochschild 2003). If the United States were to join most of the developed world and provide paid parental leave, this would go a long way in supporting breastfeeding. It should also generate support from a broad range of groups regardless of their position on breastfeeding since it is an investment in families and the future that affects a wider range of individuals.

A caring *infant feeding advocacy* that works to promote a culture where women are able to feed their children in the best possible environment is the optimal solution to the paradox in which we find ourselves. This kind of advocacy needs to be built from a dialogue across women's groups, breastfeeding advocates, the mother's movement, labor, and others. Together we can get there.

Bibliography

Afriyle, Rose. 2006. "U.S. Lacks Support for Breastfeeding Mothers." National *NOW Times*. October 2. http://www.now.org/.

Aguilar, Lauren. 2012. "The Myth of the Ideal Worker: The New Workforce, Outdated Workplace." 16 April 2012. *Gender News*. http://gender.stanford.edu/news.

American Academy of Pediatrics. 1997. "Breastfeeding and the Use of Human Milk." *Pediatrics* 100(6): 1035–39.

———. 2005. "Breastfeeding and the Use of Human Milk." *Pediatrics*. 115(2): 496–506.

———. 2012. "Breastfeeding and the Use of Human Milk." *Pediatrics*. 129(3): 827–841.

———. 2013. *Federal Support for Breastfeeding*. www2.aap.org/breastfeeding/files/pdf/federalsupportforbreastfeedingresource.pdf

Apple, Rima. 1987. *Mothers and Medicine: A Social History of Infant Feeding* 1890–1950. Madison: The University of Wisconsin Press.

Barber, Kathi. 2005. The Black Woman's Guide to Breastfeeding: The Definitive Guide to Nursing for African American Mothers. Naperville: Sourcebooks.

Barston, Suzanne. 2012. *Bottled Up: How the Way We Feed Babies Has Come To Define Motherhood and Why It Shouldn't*. Berkeley: University of California Press.

Blue Milk. 2012. "Why Breastfeeding is a Feminist Issue." *Feministe*. August 26.

Blum, Linda M. 1993. "Mothers, Babies, and Breastfeeding in Late Capitalist America: The Shifting Contexts of Feminist Theory." *Feminist Studies*. 19(2): 291–311.

———. 1999. *At the Breast*. Boston: Beacon Press.

Bobel, Christina G. "Bounded Liberation: 2001. A Focused Study of La Leche League International." *Gender and Society*. 15 (February):130–151.

———. 2002. *The Paradox of Natural Mothering*. Philadelphia: Temple University Press.

Boswell-Penc, Maia. 2006. "Tainted Milk: Breastmilk, Feminisms, and the Politics of Environmental Degradation." Albany: SUNY.

Carter, Pamela. 1995. *Feminism, Breasts, and Breast-Feeding*. New York: St. Martin's Press.

Centers for Disease Control. 2014. *Breastfeeding Report Card*. http://www.cdc.gov/breastfeedingreportcard.htm.

Centers For Disease Control. 1999. "Ten Great Public Health Achievements—United States 1900–1999." *Morbidity and Mortality Weekly Report*. Apr 2;48(12):241-3. http://www.cdc.gov/mmwr/.

Clarke, Sarah. 2014. "Should We Stop Acting Like Breastfeeding Is a Big Deal? *Best for Babes*. http://www.bestforbabes.org.

Cohn, D'Vera, Gretchen Livingston, and Wendy Wan. 2014. "After Decades of Decline, A Rise in Stay-at-Home Mothers." *Pew Research Social and Demographic. Trends*. April 8.

Connolly, Paul. 1998. "'Dancing to the Wrong Tune': Ethnography Generalization and Research on Racism in Schools." in *Researching Racism in Education: Politics, Theory, and Practice*. Edited by Paul Connolly and Barry Troyna, 122–139. Buckingham: Open University Press.

Connolly, Rachel, Deborah S. DeGraff, and Rachel A. Willis. 2004. *Kids at Work: The Value of Employer-Sponsored On-Site Child Care Centers*. Kalamazoo: W. E. Upjohn Institute for Employment Research.

Currie, Donya. 2013. "Breastfeeding Rates for Black US Women Increase, but Lag Overall: Continuing Disparity Raises Concerns." *The Nation's Health*. 43(3): 1–20.

Duany, Andres, Elisabeth Plater-Zyberk, Jeff Speck. 2000. *Suburban Nation: The Rise of Sprawl and the End of the American Dream*. New York: North Point Press.

Dunham, Ethel C. and Marian M. Crane. 1943. *Standards and Recommendations for the Hospital Care of Newborn Infants*. Washington, DC: United States Department of Labor.

Eldredge, Maureen E. 2005. "The Quest for a Lactating Male: Biology, Gender, and Discrimination." *Chicago-Kent Law Review*. 80: 875.

Employment Development Department, State of California. 2014. *Paid Family Leave: Ten Years of Assisting Californians in Need*. http://www.eddca.gov.

Ford, Dionna. 2013a. "Concord Mall Equates Breastfeeding Babies to 'Sucking on Wife's Breasts in Public'; Attempts Cover Up." Best for Babes. January 6. http://www.bestforbabes.org/concord-mall-equates-breastfeeding-babies-to-sucking-on-wifes-breasts-in-public-attempts-cover-up/.

Ford, Dionna. 2013b. "Racy Hollister Okay with Sexy Pics, not Breastfeeding for Tweens." *Best for Babes*. January 3. http://www.bestforbabes.org/breastfeeding-harassment-at-hollister-laws-offer-no-real-protection/.

Ford, Lynne. 2006. *Women and Politics: The Pursuit of Equality*. Independence: Cengage Learning.

Foster, Anneke. 2010. "Café Manager Berates Breastfeeding Mom." *ABC News*. May 13. http://abcnewsgo.com.

Galson, Steven. 2009. "The 25th Anniversary of the Surgeon General's Workshop on Breastfeeding and Human Lactation." *Public Health Reports*. 124(3): 356–358.

Galtry, Judith. 2000. "Extending the 'Bright Line': Feminism, Breastfeeding, and the Workplace in the United States." *Gender and Society*. 1(2) 295–317.

Gandy, Kim. 2006. "Open Letter to the Department of Health and Human Services Secretary Mike Leavitt." *National Organization for Women* July 19. http://www.now.org.

Gatens, Moira, 1988. "Towards a Feminist Philosophy of the Body." *In Crossing Boundaries: Feminism and the Critiques of Knowledges*. Edited by Barbara Caine et al. Sydney: Allen and Unwin.

Glendon, Mary Ann. 1991. *Rights Talk: The Impoverishment of Political Discourse*. New York: Free Press.

Goldfarb, Zachary A. 2014. "Why is Obama Having So Much Trouble Helping Working Families." *The Washington Post*. June 23. http://www.washingtonpost.com/blogs/wonkblog/wp/2014/06/23/why-obama-is-having-so-much-trouble-helping-americas-new-moms/.

Grossman, Joanna L. 2012. "The Controversy Over Public Breastfeeding: Breast May Be Best But Not In My Backyard (or Airplane)." *Verdict: Legal Analysis and Commentary from Justia*. March 20. https://verdict.justia.com/2012/03/20/the-controversy-over-public-breastfeeding.

Grumet, Jamie Lynn. 2012. "10 Things Breastfeeding Advocates Need to Stop Saying." April 4. *BlogHer*. http://www.blogher.com.

Guest, Greg, Arwen Bunce, Laura Johnson. 2006. "How Many Interviews Are Enough? An Experiment with Data Saturation and Variability." *Field Methods*. 18(1): 59–82. http://fmx.sagepub.com/content/18/1/59.

Hannan, Abeda, Sandra Benton-Davis, Laurance Grummer-Strawn. 2005. "Regional Variation in Public Opinion about Breastfeeding in the U.S." *Journal of Human Lactation*. 21 (August): 284–288.

Hausman, Bernice L. 2003. *Mother's Milk: Breastfeeding Controversies in American Culture*. New York: Routeledge.

————. 2012. "Feminism and Breastfeeding: Rhetoric, Ideology, and the Material Realities of Women's Lives." in *Beyond Health, Beyond Choice: Breastfeeding Contraints and Realities*, Edited by Paige Hall Smith, Bernice Hausman, and Miriam Labbok, 15–23. New Brunswick: Rutgers University Press.

Hochschild, Arlie Russell. 1988. *The Second Shift*. London: Penguin.

Kalma, Elita. 2010. "Breast Is Best: Where Is the Confusion?" *Blacktating*. November 5. http://www.blacktating.com.

Kay, Herma Hill. 1987. "Equality and Difference: A Perspective on No-Fault Divorce and Its Aftermath." *The University of Cincinnati Law Review*. 56(1) 1–90.

Kedrowski, Karen M. and Michael E. Lipscomb. 2008. *Breastfeeding Rights in the United States*. Westport: Praeger.

Kittay, Eva Feder. 1999. *Love's Labor.: Essays on Women, Equality, and Dependency*. New York: Routldege.

Krasny, Jill. 2012. "Every Parent Should Know the Scandalous History of Infant Formula." *Business Insider*. June 25.

La Leche League International. 2010. *The Womanly Art of Breastfeeding*. 8th Ed. New York: Random House.

————. 2004. *The Womanly Art of Breastfeeding*. 7 Ed.: Plume.

————. 1963. *The Womanly Art of Breastfeeding*. 2nd Ed. Franklin Park, Illinois: La Leche League International.

Laue, James H. 1989. *Direct Action & Desegregation, 1960–1962*. New York: Carlson Publishing Series.

Law, Jules. 2000. "The Politics of Breastfeeding: Assessing Risk, Dividing Labor." *Signs*. 25(2).

Lewin, Adrienne Mand. 2005. "Breast-feeding Moms Take Action." *ABC News*. December 29th. http://abcnews.go.com/US/Health/story?id=1378087.

Lewis, Jane and Celia Davies. 1990. "Protective Legislation in Britain: 1870–1990: Equality, Difference, and Their Implication for Women." *Policy and Politics*. 19(1): 13–25.

Ludden, Jennifer. 2014. "Family and Medical Leave Act Not Working for Many Employees. *National Public Radio*. February 5.http://www.npr.org/2013/02/05/171078451/fmla-not-really-working-for-many-employees.

Maclean, Heather. 1990. *Women's Experience of Breastfeeing*. Toronto: University of Toronto.

Marcus, Jake. 2007. "Lactation and the Law." *Mothering*. Issue 143, July/August. http://www.mothering.com/articles/lactation-and-the-law/.

————. 2010. "Curb Your Enthusiasm About the New Federal Workplace Pumping Law." *Sustainable Mothering*. May 10. http://www.sustainablemothering.com.

————. 2015. "State Laws." *Breastfeeding Law: Know Your Legal Rights*. http://www.breastfeedinglaw.com. (August 20, 2014).

Meier, Kenneth. 1994. *The Politics of Sin: Drugs, Alcohol, and Public Policy*. Armonk, NY: M. E. Sharpe.

Morran, Chris. 2014. "Victoria's Secret Apologizes After Store Tells Mom to Breastfeed in Alley." *The Consumerist*. January, 24. http://consumerist.com/2014/01/24/victorias-secret-apologizes-after-store-tells-mom-to-breastfeed-in-alley/

Muller, Mike. 1974. *The Baby Killer*. London: War on Want. http://www.waronwant.org/past-campaigns/baby-milk.

————. 2013. "The Nestle Baby Milk Scandal Has Grown Up But Not Gone Away." *The Guardian*. February 13.http://www.theguardian.com/sustainable-business/nestle-baby-milk-scandal-food-industry-standards.

Nathanson, Janice. 2012. "Maternal Activism: How Feminist Is It?" in *Feminist Mothering* Edited by Andrea O'Reilly, 243–256. Albany: SUNY Press.

National Conference of State Legislatures. 2013. "State Family and Medical Leave Laws." December 31, 2013. http://www.ncsl.org/research/labor-and-employment/state-family-and-medical-leave-laws.aspx.

————. 2015. "State Breastfeeding Laws." *National Council of State Legislatures*. March 31. http://www.ncsl.org/research/health/breastfeeding-state-laws.aspx.

National Organization for Women Foundation. 2006. *Sex-Based Discrimination in the United States.* http://www.nowfoundation.org/issues/economic/2006.

National Organization for Women. 2013. "Legislative and Workplace Actions: Mothers and Caregivers Economic Rights." http://www.now.org/mothers/legislation.html. (Accessed July 15).

Neifert, Marianne. 2001. "Prevention of Breastfeeding Tragedies." In *The Pediatric Cliniccs of North America: Breastfeeding Part II, the Management of Breastfeeding.* Edited by Richard J. Schanler. Philadelphia: W. B. Saunders Company.

Newson, John and Elizabeth. 1963. *Patterns of Infant Care in an Urban Community.* Harmondsworth: Penguin.

Norrander, Barbara. 2008. "The History of the Gender Gaps." *Voting the Gender Gap.* Edited by Lois Duke Whitiker. Urbana: University of Illinois Press.

OECD. 2009. "CO15: Breastfeeding Rates." OECD Family Database OECD Social Policy Division. Directorate of Employment, Labour and Social Affairs. http://www.oecd.org/social/family/43136964.pdf.

Oliveira, Frazão, and Smallwood. 2011. *The Infant Formula Market: Consequences of a Change in the WIC Contract Brand.*ERR 124, Economic Research Service USDA. http://www.ers.usda.gov/media/121286/err124.pdf.

Palmer, Gabrielle. 2009. *The Politics of Breastfeeding: When Breasts Are Bad for Business.* London: Pinter & Martin.

Palmer, Linda Folden. 2013. "When It Has to Be Formula: Optimizing the Health of Your Formula-Fed Baby." *The Baby Bond,* August. http://www.Babyreference.com.

Parenting in the Workplace Institute. 2014. "Executive Summary of a PIWI Babies at Work Program." *Parenting in the Workplace Institute Bringing New Life to the Workplace.* http://www.babiesatwork.org/PIWI%20Executive%20Summary.pdf.

Pateman, C. 1988. *The Sexual Contract.* Redwood City: Stanford University Press.

Perrine, Cria G., Kelly S. Scanlon, Ruowei Li, Erica Odum, and Laurence Grummer-Strawn. 2011. "Baby-Friendly Hospital Practices and Meeting Breastfeeding Intention." *Pediatrics.* 130(1): 3633.

Powell. 2008. "Balancing Act: Discourses of Feminism, Motherhood, and Activism." In *Feminist Mothering.* ed. Andrea O'Reilly, pp. 257–271. Albany: SUNY Press.

Ray, Rebecca. 2008. *A Detailed Look at Parental Leave in 21 OECD Countries.* Washington, DC: Center for Economic and Policy Research.

Reeves, Chelsea C., Fran T. Close, Mary Copeland Simmons, and Adrienne L. Hollis. 2006. "Social Support Indicators that Influence Breastfeeding Decisions in Mothers of North Florida." Florida Public Health Review. 3:1–7.

Regales, Jackie. "Nursing at Starbucks: An Interview with Lorig Charkoudian." *Hip Mamma.* http://www.Hipmamma.com.

Reneau, Annie. 2013. "What's So Hard About Covering Up to Breastfeed in Public?" *Motherhood and More.* Sunday, August 18. http://www.motherhoodandmore.com/2013/08/whats-so-hard-about-covering-up-to-html.html.

Rippeyoung, Phyllis L. F. and Mary C. Noonan. 2012. "Breastfeeding and the Gendering of Infant Care." In *Beyond Health, Beyond Choice: Breastfeeding Constraints and Realities.* Edited by Paige Hall Smith, Bernice L. Hausman, and Miriam Labbok, 133–143. New Brunswick: Rutgers University Press.

Rochman, Bonnie 2011. "Target Nurse-In: Did it Change Perceptions of Public Breast-feeding?" *Time.* December 29. http://healthland.time.com/2011/12/29/target-nurse-in-did-it-change-perceptions-of-public-breast-feeding/.

———. 2012. "Why Most Women Don't Meet Their Own Breastfeeding Goals." *Time.com.* June 4 http://healthland.time.com/2012/06/04/why-most-moms-cant-reach-their-own-breast-feeding-goals/.

Rosin, Hanna. 2009. "The Case Against Breast-Feeding." *The Atlantic Monthly* (April).

Scott, Joan W. 1988. "Deconstructing Equality-versus-Difference: Or the Uses of Post Structuralist Theory for Feminism." *Feminist Studies.* 14(1): 33-50.

Shriver, Maria. 2014. "Celebrating 10 Years of Paid Family Leave in California—Now Lets Get the Word Out!" *The Huffington Post.* July 2. http://www.huffingtonpost.com/maria-shriver/celebrating-10-years-of-paid-family-leave-in-california_b_5553292.html.

Smith, Anne. 2013. "Increasing Your Milk Supply." *Breastfeeding Basics.* October. www.breaastfeeding basics.com.

Smith, Page Hall, Bernice L. Hausman, and Miriam Labbok. 2012. *Beyond Heath, Beyond Choice: Breastfeeding Constraints and Realities.* New Brunswick: Rutgers University Press.

Solomon, Barry S., Gregory Blaschke, Daniel West, Richard Pan, Lee Sanders, Nancy Swigonski, Ernestine Willis, Donald Schwarz. 2006. "Pediatric Residents' Perceptions of Community Involvement Prior to Residency." *Ambulatory Pediatrics* 6: 337–341.

Stearns, Cindy. 1999. "Breastfeeding and the Good Maternal Body." *Gender and Society.* 13(3): 308–325.

Taylor, Erin N. 2003. "Throwing the Baby Out with the Bathwater: Childfree Advocates and the Rhetoric of Choice." *Women and Politics*, 24(4): 49–75.

Taylor, Erin N. and Lora Ebert Wallace. 2012. "Feminist Breastfeeding Promotion and the Problem of Guilt." *In Beyond Health, Beyond Choice: Breastfeeding Constraints and Realities.* Edited by Paige Hall Smith, Bernice L. Hausman, and Miriam Labbock, 193–202. New Brunswick: Rutgers University Press.

Tronto, Joan. 2013. *Caring Democracy: Markets, Equality, and Justice.* New York: NY University Press.

Tucker, Judith Stadtman. 2012. "Rocking the Boat: Feminism and the Ideological Grounding of the Twenty-First Century Mother." In *Feminist Mothering.* Edited by Andrea O'Reilly, 205–218. Albany: SUNY Press.

U.S. Department of Health and Human Services. 2011a. *Doctors in Action: A Call to Action From the Surgeon General to Support Breastfeeding.* http://monadnockcommunityhospital.com/pdf/mpinc/doctors_in_action.pdf.

U.S. Department of Health and Human Services. 2011b. *Executive Summary: The Surgeon General's Call to Action to Support Breastfeeding.* http://www.surgeongeneral.gov/library/calls/breastfeeding/calltoactiontosupportbreastfeeding.pdf.

United Nations International Children's Emergency Fund. 2014. "The Baby-Friendly Hospital Initiative." November 10. http://www.unicef.org/programme/breastfeeding/baby.htm.

United States Breastfeeding Committee. 2011. *State Breastfeeding Legislation.* http://www.usabreastfeeding.org.

———. 2012. "Joint letter to the Editor of *TIME*: We are All Mom Enough and We Call a Truce." May 16. http://www.usbreastfeeding.org.

———. 2013. "Recent USBC Activities and Accomplishments." http://www.usbreastfeeding.org/AboutUs/RecentActivitiesAccomplishments/tabid/63/Default.aspx2015.

Urban, Annie. 2012. "Why Women Don't Meet Their Breastfeeding Goals." *Care2.* June 12. http://www.care2.com.

Vance, Melissa. 2005. "Breastfeeding Legislation in the United States: A General Overview and Implications for Helping Mothers." Reprinted from *LEAVEN.* 41(3): 51–54. http://www.llli.org/llleaderweb/lv/lvjunjul05p51.html.

Van Esterik, Penny. 1989. *Beyond the Breast-Bottle Controversy.* New Brunswick, NJ: Rutgers University Press.

Van Esterick, Penny. 1995. "The Politics of Breastfeeding: An Advocacy Perspective" in *Breastfeeding: Biocultural Perspectives.* Edited by Patricia Stuart Macadam and Katherine A. Detwyler. Hawthorne: Walter de Gruyter, Inc.

Waring, Marilyn. 1990. *If Women Counted: A New Feminist Economics.* New York: HarperCollins Publishers.

Ward, Jule DeJager. 2000. *Le Leche League: at the Crossroads of Medicine, Feminism, and Religion.* Chapel Hill: University of North Carolina Press.

Whelan, Brianne. 2005. "For Crying Out Loud: Ohio's Legal Battle with Public Breastfeeding and Hope for the Future." *American University Journal of Gender, Social Policy & the Law.* 13: 669.

Wiessinger, Diane. 1996. "Watch Your Language." *The Journal of Human Lactation.* Vol. 12 No. 1.

Wight, Nancy E. 2001. "Management of Common Breastfeeding Issues." *The Pediatric Clinics of North America Breastfeeding 2001, Part II The Management of Breastfeeding*. Edited by Richard J. Schanler. Philadelphia: W. B. Saunders Company.

Williams, Joan 2000. *Unbending Gender: Why Family and Work Conflict and What to Do About It*. New York: Oxford University Press

Wolf, Jacqueline. 2003. "Low Breastfeeding Rates and Public Health in the United States." *American Journal of Public Health*. 93(12).

———. 2008. "Got Milk? Not in Public!" *International Breastfeeding Journal*. 31(2): 397–424.

Wolf, Joan. 2007. "Is Breast Really Best? Risk and Total Motherhood in the National Breast-feeding Awareness Campaign." *Journal of Health Politics, Policy, and Law*, 32(4): 596–636 (2007), 595–36.

———. 2011. *Is Breast Best? Taking on the Breastfeeding Experts and the New High Stakes of Motherhood*. New York: New York University Press.

Woliver, Laura. 1993. *From Outrage to Action: The Politics of Grass-Roots Dissent*. Urbana: University of Illinois Press.

———. 2002. *The Political Geographies of Pregnancy*. Urbana: University of Illinois Press.

Wykes, Julia. 2014. "The Disturbing Trend I Noticed When My Breastfeeding Story Went Viral." *The Huffington Post*. July 2.

Wright, Anne L. 2001. "The Rise of Breastfeeding in the United States." The Pediatric Clinics of North America Breastfeeding 2001, Part II The Management of Breastfeeding. Edited by Richard J. Schanler. Philadelphia: W. B. Saunders Company.

Wright, Anne and Richard Schanler. 2001. "The Resurgence of Breastfeeding at the End of the Second Millennium." *The Journal of Nutrition*. 131(2): 421S–425S.

Young, Iris Marion. 1990. *Justice and the Politics of Difference*. Princeton, NJ: Princeton University Press.

Appendix A

Orin C. Smith, President, CEO, Director
Starbucks Coffee Company
P.O. Box 3717
Seattle, WA 98124-3717

Dear Mr. Smith:

My name is _____ and I am ___ months old. I like to drink my mama's breast milk. It tastes good and it is so good for me. I like the fact that when my mama takes me places, she feeds me when I am hungry, which is a lot, since my tummy is so small. Sometimes she goes to Starbucks. When she does, I don't want to be hungry. I want to be able to nurse there, too. I don't like nursing under a blanket because I can't see my mama and my mama can't see me and it gets hot and uncomfortable under there. I really don't like nursing in the bathroom. That's gross. Do you like to eat your food in the bathroom?

Please make a policy so that no one will ever ask my mama to stick a blanket over my head or take me in the bathroom to nurse.

Thank you.

Sincerely,

Appendix A

NOTES

Source: Letter from Lorig Charkoudian's webpage was posted at http://www.nurseatstarbucks. org/ Accessed April 1, 2006.

Appendix B

2005 Testimony Before Senate Public Health and Welfare Committee

For

Representative Sharp
Dr. Brendan Kennedy, MD Pediatrics
Brenda Bandy, La Leche League
Julie Quinn
Theresa Wiegel, La Leche League
Kelley Stuppy

Opposed

Kathy Porter, Kansas Office of Judicial Registration (opposed to jury duty exemption only)

2005 Letters in Support of HB 2284 to House Health and Human Services Committee

Karen Meek, R.N.
Emily Regan, Dept. of Biochemistry, KSU
Pat Olson
Lara Williams, IBCLC (International Board Certified Lactation Consultant)
Frank and Florena Schneweis

Mary Honas, La Leche League member
Cheryl Peachey Stoner, La Leche League Leader
Dawn Hawkins
Laura McComb
Seanna L. East, R.N.
Christie Pate, OTR, IBCLC
Melissa Peat
Stacy Tidmore, PhD

Submitted Testimony to House

Danielle Huckins, March of Dimes, Greater Kansas Chapter
Kansas State Nurses Association

Appendix C

2006 Testimony Before Senate Public Health and Welfare Committee

For

Amy Swan, Nursing Mother, Kansas Constituent
Agatha Nickelson, Nursing Mother, Kansas Constituent
Libby Rosen, R.N. KAW Area Breastfeeding Coalition
Bob Swan, Father of Amy Swan, Kansas Consituent
Brenda Bandy, La Leche League of Kansas
Susan Bumsted, R.N. Kansas State Nurses Association

2006 Written Testimony Submitted to Senate Public Health and Welfare Committee

Linda Kenny, KDHE (Kansas Department of Health and Environment)
Karen Brubaker, BSN, R.N.
Angela Taylor, Nursing Mother, Kansas Constituent
Jessica Rau, Nursing Mother, Kansas Constituent
Leah Garver, Nursing Mother, Kansas Constituent
Kelly Hawkins Skinner, Nursing Mother, Kansas Constituent
Debra Welty, R.N.
Jane Graves, Nursing Mother, Kansas Constituent

Index

CPSIA information can be obtained at www.ICGtesting.com
Printed in the USA
BVOW08*1221250615

405843BV00003B/4/P